Equivocal Endings in Classic American Novels

Hester Prynne: a painting by Sigismond De Iranowski
for *The Century Magazine*, 1912.

Equivocal Endings in Classic American Novels

The Scarlet Letter;
Adventures of Huckleberry Finn;
The Ambassadors; The Great Gatsby

JOYCE A. ROWE

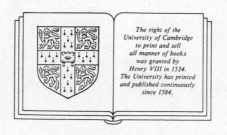

The right of the
University of Cambridge
to print and sell
all manner of books
was granted by
Henry VIII in 1534.
The University has printed
and published continuously
since 1584.

Cambridge University Press

Cambridge
New York   Port Chester   Melbourne   Sydney

Published by the Press Syndicate of the University of Cambridge
The Pitt Building, Trumpington Street, Cambridge CB2 1RP
40 West 20th Street, New York, NY 10011, USA
10 Stamford Road, Oakleigh, Melbourne 3166, Australia

© Cambridge University Press 1988

First published 1988
Reprinted 1988, 1989

Printed in Great Britain at
the Athenaeum Press Ltd, Newcastle upon Tyne

British Library cataloguing in publication data

Rowe, Joyce A.
Equivocal endings of classic American
novels: The scarlet letter, Adventures of
Huckleberry Finn, The ambassador, The
great Gatsby.
1. American fiction — 19th century —
History and criticism. 2. American fiction
— 20th century — History and criticism
I. Title
813'.009 PS377

Library of Congress cataloguing in publication data

Rowe, Joyce A.
Equivocal endings of classic American novels.
Bibliography.
Includes index.
1. American fiction — History and criticism.
2. Closure (Rhetoric). 3. Ambiguity in literature.
I. Title
PS374.C56R68 1988 813'.009 87-15868

ISBN 0 521 33532 9

For
Claudia, Nina and Gerry

Contents

Acknowledgments

This book began as a doctoral dissertation written under the direction of Quentin Anderson, now Professor Emeritus of Columbia University. It gives me great pleasure and pride to express my debt to him. His commitments, judgments and deep learning have taught me what humanistic scholarship and criticism can mean. Despite the pressure of his own responsibilities, he has been selfless in his attention to the entirety of this project. Rigorous as he is kind and caring, his challenges have enlivened my work and sustained my spirit at every turn.

Readers of this work may recognize how much I also owe to Sacvan Bercovitch, an inspiriting and generous teacher, whose powerful ideas about American culture have stimulated me to explore new perspectives on many traditional themes. Professor Bercovitch has kindly read and commented upon part of this manuscript. Werner Sollors saw the manuscript in its initial stages and offered much valuable advice. Carl Hovde has been an astute reader throughout. His suggestions and commentary have been extremely helpful.

I would like to express very special thanks to Jack Salzman, Director of the Center for American Culture Studies, Columbia University. His judgment and enthusiasm made it possible to transform an academic dissertation into a book.

For a grant from the Elliott V. K. Dobbie Fund to aid in preparing the manuscript for publication, I am grateful to the Graduate Department of English and Comparative Literature, Columbia University.

Finally, I want to applaud my family for their unflagging good cheer and self-reliance, for respecting my long hours of solitude, and for their spontaneous faith that the free mind provides its own reward.

Introduction

I

To the passionate reader, the ending of a good story is a mixed blessing. For though we demand endings to confirm or complete our sense of relations within a story and so make a work fully signify, an ending, like its real life counterpart, also entails a sense of loss, of emptiness – a little death, as it were. In this sense, fictional endings, whatever their ostensible resolution, are inherently equivocal. In fulfilling our desire for a world of "charged meanings" and singular events they recapitulate the wisdom of Prospero – reminding us that the meaning we seek is a vision we impose; that our finest aspirations are generated from the "baseless [and varied] fabric" of our dreams.[1]

Shakespeare's *The Tempest* is associated with the Elizabethan voyages to the New World and the utopian ideals rekindled by its discovery.[2] But when Prospero breaks his staff, resigns his powers, and returns to the world of the Renaissance state, he confirms his audience (and their English descendants) in a more restrictive sense of human possibility, and reality, than that which their American cousins were to evolve on their side of the Atlantic ocean. For despite cross-currents and interpenetrating influences between the two continents, by the mid-nineteenth century when, it is generally recognized, American writers had found their own style and voice, their formal as well as thematic concerns were generating a decidedly different literature from that produced by comparable writers abroad.

Nowhere, perhaps, is this more evident than in the pattern of the endings of classic American novels and their troubling relation to the narrative which precedes them. These endings are equivocal in a special thematic sense, as they simultaneously promote and deny a visionary ambition already defeated in the body of the work. Neither tragic, comic nor ironic, they are, rather deliberately evasive, eluding those truths of experience, of both self and world, which the preceding narrative has been at pains to establish. What is most telling about this pattern is that it can be shown to persist in works which represent disparate styles and genres – works which were written both pre- and post-Civil War, and which thus span a paradigmatic historical era in which Americans were absorbing, at an unprecedented rate, social, economic, and political changes. These changes, one might think, would radically redefine the experience of what it means to be an American. Yet the thematic and structural consistency in these books suggests otherwise. At the deepest level, there seems to be no significant alteration in the conceptual pattern by which our major artists have perceived and interpreted our culture's dominant themes.

Each of these works is focussed on a protagonist whose visionary longings separate him or her from direct engagement with common social experience. Regularly figured as a society *à deux*, a bond of ideal love or brotherhood which can only exist outside the given social order, the protagonist's vision challenges a morally inadequate reality which, nevertheless, consumes his or her attention as it stimulates his or her resistance. In the course of the tale, the idealist is defeated, as much by his or her own limitations as by the society at hand. Yet these endings all adhere to a similar convention: they redeem or rehabilitate the ideal by recasting it in alternative terms. However equivocally it is stated, the protagonist refuses either to reconsider or to abandon visionary hope. In effect, he or she refuses to learn anything about self or world from the experiences undergone in the course of the story. Why this should be – and what species of narrative logic or illogic allows the reader to share in the affect of these endings, making plausible or convincing what, empirically, ought to be neither – will be the main theme of this book. Once formulated, these issues inevitably suggest the pressure of a cultural imperative to which both writer and reader are subtly bound.

In recent decades a good deal of critical attention has been devoted to the subject of literary endings. It is clear that the convention, in its varied guises, embodies deeply felt human needs. Frank Kermode has related the endings in Western literary tradition to the great apocalyptic paradigms of Judaeo-Christian culture. He finds that these types continue to "underlie ways of making sense of the world from where we stand, in the middest."[3] Other critical studies have examined forms of the ending in relation to unresolved tensions generated within an individual work, within the consciousness of an individual character, or as a structural key to retrospective interpretation of the whole text.[4]

While each of these studies offers valuable insights into a complex subject, my own interest lies in the question of how a particular culture adapts and defines traditional expressive patterns to its own needs and purposes. I want to state at the outset what may appear as a truism to some readers, but which, perhaps for this reason, is often ignored in practice by literary specialists and educated readers alike. This is the recognition that writers are, like the rest of us, inevitably shaped by those forms of thought and feeling, and modes of interpreting experience, which constitute the outline of what we have come to define as a cultural (as well as personal) form of identity. If, as Clifford Geertz puts it, "men unmodified by the customs of a particular place do not in fact exist," then we must be consistent in our attempt to understand the depth and range of a writer's potential engagement with his or her culture's dominant themes.[5] I intend by this something more than the traditional determination of "influence," historical and/or biographical. What I'm concerned with is how a writer assimilates, accommodates to and struggles for dominion over those persistent themes and values that embody what Geertz defines as the core of culture: "the attainment of concepts, the apprehension and application of specific systems of symbolic meaning," which serve as "plans, recipes . . . instructions . . . for the governing of behavior."[6] Thus my emphasis will be not on literary structure *per se*, but on how structure establishes and controls meaning – defining thematic relations, denying one option, enforcing another – and so illuminates an author's conflicting commitments and concerns.

Let me then begin my examination of the American sense of an ending by stressing certain aspects of what I take to be the cultural ideology which informs these novels and the major structural patterns they share.

II

For Americans, the period from the 1850s to the 1920s, which these books span, is commonly accounted one of great energy, confidence, and optimism about the future. Despite armed conflict and social upheaval, Americans were perennially reminded that the

3

blessings of material prosperity which accompanied industrial and geographic expansion confirmed their special status among nations – not merely a nascent continental power with abundant resources, but mankind's last best hope.[7]

That Americans, from the Puritan migration onward, have seen themselves and their country as participants in a unique social and spiritual enterprise is, indeed, basic to the rhetoric of our national life. In the expanding polity of the nineteenth century, no voice had more cultural resonance than that of Ralph Waldo Emerson. Emerson's early essays formulate a new relation between the moral and spiritual ambition inherited from the old Puritan theocracy and the gospel of individual equality endemic to the Jacksonian era. His republic of the spirit, in which each, paradoxically, becomes the equal of all, defined a new creed of democratic idealism – one that many scholars believe continues, in various guises, to influence American attitudes toward self and community today.[8]

However, the standard conception of Emerson's influence on American culture continues to emphasize a split between the Emersonian tradition and "a counter tradition originating in opposition to him."[9] For though Emerson is regularly given his due as the spiritual mentor of Thoreau and Whitman, his role is not recognized as frequently for the way it permeates, or at least is congruent with, that image of the American self which can be found in all our classic novelists, regardless of which side of the Emersonian dialectic one places them on.

Emerson's early essays, especially "Nature" and "The American Scholar," can serve to preface what I take to be the major ideological concern of all the novels under discussion here. In radical opposition to the traditional view which sees institutional forces – religious, social, familial – as the shapers of individual identity, Emerson posits a new, self-created man who takes the measure of himself, not from his interaction with others, past and present, but from a visionary act, based upon a spiritualized interpretation of nature.[10] Nature, as the emanation of spirit, becomes, in effect, the double of the soul. Relying upon a greatly expanded version of conscience, an inner truth patterned on the sublime coherence of the cosmos, Emerson asks, "Who can set bounds to the possibilities of man?"[11] The redeemed soul is one whose vision can "read" and so "possess" the landscape; who can, in effect, re-imagine it as an

4

inexhaustible metaphor for his own state of being. As nature is shown to furnish man with a storehouse of analogies for his moral guidance, so it infuses him with a sense of vast, impersonal, and ever-renewable spiritual power. Thus conceived, it becomes the ground for a new, self-validating identity with transcendent implications. The totality of this new faith allows Emerson to proclaim that man has it in him to create the world anew. In a secular version of millennial salvation, he promises that "As fast as you go on to conform your life to the pure idea in your mind" all disagreeable things shall disappear: "Pests, madhouses, prisons, enemies [shall] vanish . . . Until evil is no more seen."[12]

Among its many radical implications, Emerson's rhetoric is notable for the way in which the new man and the new society appear as one and the same. As Sacvan Bercovitch has demonstrated, Emerson took the Romantic concept of the inspired perceiver and adjusted its tenets to the rhetoric of America's special destiny, passed on from the Puritan errand. The self he sought in the American landscape was both personal and national, representative of an ideal America to be. In this sense the landscape itself was "the text of America, simultaneously an external model of perfection and a product of the symbolic imagination." As its title emphasizes, "The American Scholar" outlines a vision of self-perfection that simultaneously prophesies a "New World future."[13]

Thus Emerson can assure his audience that if the new man, the American, would "plant himself indomitably on his instincts and there abide, the huge world will come round to him."[14] This American Colossus bestriding his "narrow world" provides us with an image that seems to epitomize the strenuous necessity under which democratic idealism labors: the demand that individual identity conform to the same morally ambitious pattern as that asserted in the older national claim to exemplary status. In Emerson (and even more in Thoreau and Whitman) this unitary aspiration is characterized by a cosmic optimism that seems calculated to dissolve the boundary between public and private, individual and social aspects of experience. As "the currents of the Universal Being circulate" through him, says Emerson, "all mean egotism vanishes."[15] Subject merges with object; man expands to the proportions of the cosmos; and, momentarily at least, self and world seem to be reborn together.

Given the "optative mood" of this ambition, it is not surprising that, as F. O. Matthiessen pointed out over forty years ago, it should have provoked an immediate counter-statement.[16] In the works of Melville and Hawthorne, each of whom insisted on an aspect of "the power of blackness" in understanding the whole of man's nature (and therefore the limited prospects for psychic and social renewal), we find, at the outset of this cultural dialogue, the most complex response to the meaning of American aspiration. Their explorations of the siren song of a regenerate or redemptive American self established a pattern of attraction and repulsion to which all the novels in this study are, I believe, indebted.

Yet, to observe that the novels to which we most attend as American classics take the negative or skeptical side in the dialogue of American moral ambition is to be struck all the more by the fact that in each ending the protagonist reaffirms some version of that aspiration which has already been defeated in the body of the narrative. As will become clear, I do not find in this pattern anything like the popular 'happy ending' of sentimental romance.[17] The novels I am concerned with afford us no version of the traditional comic resolution wherein discord is banished and social harmony restored. Nor, conversely, do they conclude with that tragic resolution in which man comes to accept his place in an impenetrable but nevertheless coherent metaphysical order. Indeed, at the close of these books, we see only as Prince Amerigo sees at the end of James's *The Golden Bowl*, when he tells the luminous Maggie, "I see nothing but *you*."[18] As a counterforce to vision, reality – as we have known it in the course of the story – has been dismissed.

These endings cannot really be considered 'open' in any of the senses usually associated with this term. Although connotations vary, there is a consensus that an open ending signifies an *openness* to experience as indeterminate and unpredictable – a flux which will never yield a permanent or stable sense of self. But the endings I am concerned with resist such a Romantic recognition and such an implied future for the idealist or his surrogate. At the close of their books, we do not find these protagonists going forward to encounter that "reality of experience" which will feed or shape vision. The notion of experience as a positive value (always a tentative one) has been jettisoned in favor of an equivocal hope.

For this reason, genre criticism, which attempts to explain

Introduction

the anomalies of American fiction by attributing them to the limitations of one or another literary mode (romance or novel), seems inadequate to account for the narrative concerns explored. Instead, I believe that the tension in these endings, taken together with the rejection of Romantic aspiration in the body of the stories, justifies a critical approach that eschews the strait-jacket of formal literary categories and concentrates instead on what, for want of a better term, I can only call narrative logic; that is, the relation of structural and thematic patterns to a work's overall implications, considered in the light of its author's cultural concerns.[19]

Without attempting to blur their individual richness or elide their significant differences, analysis yields the outline of a remarkably similar strategy at work in all these books. None of them completes the rejection of visionary aspiration, which narrative logic might lead us to expect; neither does any fully affirm that faith in exalted possibilities which has moved the protagonist onward. Rather, these endings contrive to keep vision aloft by a shift in focus and a transposition of values. Instead of that self-recognition which we might expect from the protagonist at the climax of his or her adventures, and which is the classic prelude to any significant accommodation to social reality, these characters, in varying degrees, follow the pattern of Hawthorne's Young Goodman Brown at the Devil's altar – at the moment of crisis they turn away. Protected from confronting their own limitations and nature, and from an accommodation to that shared human condition out of which all social decency derives, their attention shifts elsewhere – to the future, to the past or to another locale (inward or outward) in space or time.

Just as each of these books posits at or near its beginning an ideal image of social and moral freedom, of spiritual adventure, each ends with a protagonist alone on an empty stage, a spiritual orphan cast back once again into a metaphoric, if not literal, wilderness. In keeping with traditional associations, this virgin wilderness suggests a limbo, a place from which rebirth or renewal may yet occur. Given the quality of postponement or evasion which these endings entail, their ultimate effect is to preserve the image of a hero who is even more of a mystery at the end of his story than he was during its course. His unmasking is never completed for to do this would destroy the possibility of renewing the

7

dream, of recreating a self commensurate with the promise of a new society.

The correlatives of this pattern can be found within the structure of each text. All of these books are remarkable for their lack of a middle ground. None affords the kind of dialectical interaction between characters of opposing types, classes or attitudes that readings of English and/or Continental novels would lead us to expect. Nowhere do we find those interlinked social contexts that foster the development of personality within the moral texture of a richly nuanced world. To this end I will compare works by Dickens and Conrad with American ones, and allude to other English and Continental examples in order to clarify the implications for American identity of what Lionel Trilling called the "isolate autonomy" of the characters in American novels.[20]

For it seems clear, notwithstanding the complaints of Hawthorne, Cooper, and James that American life lacked social interest and texture, that the concerns of our major writers inhibited the depiction of a social scene which might meliorate or engross the moral energies of their protagonists. Alternative commitments, rather than the thinness of social actuality, would seem to have been the primary reason for the abstractions and polarizations which dominate the structure of these books. Hawthorne's claims in this regard are telling. What he longed for and found lacking in American life was not greater social density of the type he admired in Trollope's work, for instance, but more possibilities for a Romantic or Gothic setting: the shadow and gloom of antiquity, old and picturesque wrongs.[21] In other words, a scene that would function primarily for symbolic not mimetic purposes.

Early in this century, D. H. Lawrence, in his seminal study of American classics, claimed that American writers (like all Americans) dreamed of an anti-social, anti-humanist freedom – a desire to slough off what for Europeans constituted the sense of personal consciousness and escape into a state of being as isolate and impersonal as the new continent itself. "That is, in the progressive American consciousness there has been the one dominant desire, to do away with the old thing."[22] Lawrence may have overstated and simplified the issues, but his intuition that what can be distinguished as abstract or impersonal in the American consciousness represents a positive valence rather than merely a lack or inadequacy when measured by European standards, draws atten-

Introduction

tion to key elements of the American scene, and is still, I believe, the generative insight for comprehending these works.

One recent permutation of Lawrence's thesis which accounts in its own way for the absence of a social middle ground in key American works, and which has particular bearing on this study, is Richard Poirier's *A World Elsewhere*. Poirier discusses the style of American novelists against the foil of the English, in order to show that the latter's idea of society as a field for self-realization doesn't occur to American writers because their attention is engaged not by the possibilities for the self that exist within the social framework but by an alternative dream of boundless imaginative freedom. Thus, the world that would match this ideal state of consciousness is, by definition, elsewhere.

It would seem that the Emersonian aspiration which runs through these novels and is resurrected in their endings can, in part, be conceived in Poirier's terms. Yet the structure of these books, as well as the equivocation in their endings, suggests a more complex relation to social and psychological reality than his view permits. For in each story there seems to be more at stake than solely the struggle of the inner consciousness to break free of the prison house of daily existence. As Poirier himself points out in relation to *Huckleberry Finn*, the examination and criticism of "the social panorama" of the shore occupies a dominant portion of that book[23] – and this pattern holds true for each of the novels under discussion here.

Indeed, it is the failure of the social group to realize its communal potential that drives each of these protagonists into a deeper opposition to things as they are. For though the content of the hero's vision has been notoriously difficult to define, the structure of these books, with their emblematic partnerships, shows it to have social as well as personal ramifications. Far from being a blueprint for social or spiritual Utopia, the hero's aspiration creates the outline of an absence, an ideal defined in terms of a lack. And while each of these books provides its own historically specific commentary on the substance of this lack, taken together they express an ambition for the American self that is, I believe, both tougher and more melancholy than that self-perpetuating aesthetic exuberance, which is the goal, as Poirier sees it, of a consciousness dedicated to "boundless freedom." Indeed, by limiting himself to a study of style – the language by which private

9

consciousness seeks to evade the bounds of the social world – Poirier, though deeply sensitive to the implications of language, nevertheless himself evades consideration of the hero's complex relation to that social world which is condemned for betraying him.[24] Ultimately, the desire for a kind of gaseous expansion of consciousness, without any significant moral ballast, can all too easily be re-conceived as a longing for that perpetual adolescence which Leslie Fiedler considers to be the hallmark of American literary heroes.[25]

While there is undeniable truth to Fiedler's accusations, the condition they depict is, I believe, the result not the cause of social disaffection. What saves these books and these heroes from mere regression is the moral scrutiny they bring to bear on the society they oppose. Viewed from the perspective of their Puritan patrimony, it cannot be entirely coincidental that these works of fiction bear some faint resemblance to the effect and even the gross outline of the New England jeremiad, as they chronicle the failures of the present in the light of an ideal which they continue to resurrect.[26] Indeed, this prophetic legacy may even afford a clue to the provenance of that singular tension between individual and group which characterizes these works.

Each of these narratives is centered on a protagonist who appears as outcast or outsider to the norms of the social group with which he or she is peripherally allied. Each has an allegiance to a moral or spiritual imperative, an ideal identity (conceived as a form of freedom) which he or she asserts as an absolute, prior to any current mode of self-definition which the group may take for its own. But though the protagonist would seem to be only fortuitously connected to the group at hand, close reading suggests that there is actually a polar opposition between the two, and that at the core they are intimately allied. In each instance the protagonist remains loyal to an aspiration that the group has either abandoned or betrayed.[27] This configuration, which is keyed to motifs of disguise, secrecy and submerged leadership, is explicit in the ending of *The Scarlet Letter*, where Hester's isolation and suffering endow her with charismatic status in the eyes of the townspeople, especially the women. But versions of this basic pattern – the hero who is invested with special abilities and has a mysterious attraction for others while keeping his nature partly hidden (from himself as well as from them) – are a constant among all these books.

Introduction

And just as this protagonist represents forgotten possibilities for the group, so the group represents certain repressed or dissociated aspects of the protagonist's own nature. In each case the hero, though strong and appealing, is presented as complex and/or flawed, trapped by realities of self and circumstance which inevitably confound visionary goals.

Central to both structure and theme in these novels is the principle of divided consciousness: characters who, in reflecting suppressed aspects of one another, demonstrate the degree to which each remains a stranger to significant portions of his own identity. It is for this reason that I have chosen Hawthorne's short story "My Kinsman, Major Molineux" as a paradigm for this study. For I believe it to be the most dramatic exploration in our nineteenth-century literature of the meaning of this self-division to the American consciousness.

Although the theme of self-division is tantamount to a definition of the Romantic ethos, in less self-conscious formulations it is virtually as old as literature itself. What is notable about the American version is the manner in which it is deployed to restrict the hero's growth as well as disarm the reader's judgment. A protagonist arrives at the brink of self-confrontation only to evade it by rejecting that aspect of self which would inevitably delimit the boundaries of vision. Lambert Strether, having seen the old world for what it is and the new for what it has become, manages to free himself from both without confronting the disturbing complexity of his own emotions. But is he more or less human for the journey? While the oppositions between and within characters multiply opportunities for self-recognition, they eventually serve to stifle it. From the perspective of the ending one is forced to read back into the body of the text more authorial allegiance to the vision than these stories minus their endings would warrant.

Moreover, it is these multiple forms of self-separation that, I believe, sustain the polarities of real and ideal on which these books are structured. The masked or disguised identity which assures the hero's distance from the social scene effectively prevents that interaction with others on which, as we have noted, genuine individuality depends. To hinder the formation of an adequate middle ground within the book's structure is a strategy that enforces the power of radical imperatives, even in failure. It stimulates an expectation which only a return to the visionary mode of the ending can satisfy. "Exiles feed on empty dreams of hope," says Aeschylus's Aegisthus. And to the end, each of these protagonists remains an exile, not only from the common affections of others, but from vital aspects of his or her own nature. So Huck refuses to grow up, preferring night memories of intermittent kindness to daylight exposure in a world where the civilized and the brutal are discomfortingly twinned; and Gatsby martyrs himself, denying the raw truths of his own life in order to keep faith with a long-dead illusion.

It is telling that despite the consistency of the convention none of these endings has avoided provoking dissatisfaction, puzzlement, or dismay on the part of readers and critics. Yet, as far as I know, each has been discussed only as reflecting problems or conflicts specific to its individual author. The largest and most contentious body of critical discussion is that surrounding the final chapters of *Huckleberry Finn*. But the significance of Hester Prynne's last years – why does she return to Boston? What is her final vision meant to portend? – and the evaluation of Dimmesdale's dying confession have also led to many opposing interpretations of *The Scarlet Letter*. Lambert Strether's final choice has not only evoked conflicting views of *The Ambassadors* but of its author's character and qualities of judgment as well. Nor is Gatsby laid to rest by Nick's elegiac praise. While some critics see Gatsby as an essentially innocent or Adamic hero, accepting Nick's own judgment, others question the moral credibility of Fitzgerald's narrator and, therefore, the conclusions he draws. In short, it seems clear that a convention which recurs as regularly as this one has something to tell us, not only about the ideals by which we measure ourselves and the social cost incurred, but also about the dynamics of narrative – the strategies by which the reader's emotion is aroused and a cultural dream sustained. What we have in our fiction, I believe, is an anomaly as strangely inclusive as the country itself: stories that ratify what they seem to deny, that continue to insist, in the face of complex and contradictory evidence, on the redemptive power of the dream.

In fact, it seems that as we progress in time the pattern I am tracking becomes more rigidly insistent, the recoil from reality more perverse. There is a fictive thread to be traced from Melville's Bartleby to Mailer's Gary Gilmore; from the stoic resistance of the virtuous alien to that of the pathologically unfit. Those who

Introduction

are psychologically unable to make a social accommodation now fascinate us as much as those who once preferred not to. However, the purposes of this study are, I believe, well served by concentrating on the works of four major writers, which not only represent a canon of American self-images and values, but a long enough span of historical time to give point to the argument of a culturally consistent pattern. The writers are Nathaniel Hawthorne, Mark Twain, Henry James, and F. Scott Fitzgerald.

I

Nathaniel Hawthorne:
"My Kinsman, Major Molineux":
The Several Voices of Independence

On they went, in counterfeited pomp, in senseless uproar, in frenzied merriment, trampling all on an old man's heart.

The fundamental analogy between the forces that shape individual being and those that move history onward is, I believe, the central concern of Hawthorne's major work. Nowhere does he examine the dynamic of this connection between individual and community with such dramatic compression and specificity of its American terms as in his early tale, "My Kinsman, Major Molineux."[1] Here we have an image of the dark side of "elsewhere" – the Hades of the rebellious young American soul. This story is perhaps Hawthorne's most successful effort to fuse symbolic and allegorical modes of expression in a dramatic rendering of the interconnections among psychological, moral, and historical realms of truth. The tale, set in a context of colonial protest against Crown-imposed governors of Massachusetts Bay, seems to conflate events of the 1730s with those of the 1760s and 1770s.[2] But the hallucinatory atmosphere of the narrative transmutes given facts and historical allusions into a series of symbolic experiences which illuminate the subjective meaning of revolution and establish its role in determining the future contours of the American self.[3]

Yet, despite the extraordinary imaginative control which the tale exhibits, I find in the ending an unwillingness to complete the narrative's thematic implications. Artfully seamless in its relation to the preceding drama, the ending nevertheless permits young Robin, whose appearance and name signify the budding self-sufficiency of the young country, to evade a full recognition of who and what he is.[4] Because the tale anticipates so definitively thematic concerns and narrative strategies of the novels to be discussed, it can be used as a paradigm of the pattern I am tracing.

Powerful as a single creation, it grows even more so when we see how close its links are to preoccupations in American literature persisting through almost a century (if not more) of great societal change.

Although the story does not focus attention on any social ideal beyond the proto-revolutionary moment, this itself is conceived with all the intensity of a primal vision – a feverish dream ultimately aimed at the radical overthrow of traditional social and legal authority, embodied in the surrogate father-king figure of Major Molineux.[5] Moreover, since Robin is portrayed as a Franklinian materialist, he shares in the ethos which was later to emerge as Emersonian idealism. Jesse Bier has pointed out how these two forces are connected at the root. As the quintessential "ethical capitalist," Franklin served as a "functional historical model" for Emerson and Thoreau. "Both Franklin and Emerson deemphasized evil and were committed to beneficence." "Self-Reliance," says Bier, can be read as a transmutation of Franklin's self-help thesis. And Michael Gilmore finds in "Self-Reliance" an analogy between the merchant's economy and the soul's.[6] Thus Robin serves as prototype for all those ambitions comprised in the self-reliant ideology dominant in Hawthorne's own day – an ideology whose tendencies were confirmed in the traumatic break with the past, which Hawthorne's tale envisions as the Revolution's problematical, if not primary, legacy.

It has also been pointed out that the tale seems to have been written in reaction to the semi-centennial celebrations of 1826, which portrayed the Revolution as a calm and majestic process, a glorious fulfillment of that American destiny prefigured in the establishment of the Puritan settlements.[7] And surely among the narrative's many ironies, we may educe the outline of a salient paradox: for the crowd's violent rejection of any natural bond with the past belies the principle of linkage between type and fulfillment, past, present and future, so important to American political mythology.

In presenting us with a direct indictment of the cruelty of unchecked radical energies, Hawthorne reveals a profound skepticism toward that larger vision of social and political harmony, based on Enlightenment theories of natural rights, which justifies the claims of individualism to advance or perfect society. Robin's nostalgic reverie on the church steps, occurring just before the climactic, mutinous Saturnalia, conflates images of eighteenth-century natural religion with those of the older New England piety to suggest the abyss which divides the idyllic myths of the past from the nightmare of history he is about to encounter.

In this reverie, Robin sees the rays of the setting sun fall on a giant oak, beneath which his clergyman father is leading the family in an outdoor service of evening prayer. As the service ends and the family disappear indoors, Robin foresees his exclusion from all that "home" means: those religious, social, and political bonds which once sustained the individual in an organic community where past and future were joined under the guidance of a benevolent patriarchal order. Ultimately, what this tale reveals is the anomie and self-dissociation that result from the overthrow of such a traditional mode of authority, dramatically embodied in Robin's humiliated kinsman and pseudo-patron, the Major. The climactic tableau enacts the fearful uncertainty of a future in which self and community will be joined, not in the golden glow of a peaceable kingdom, but in the red and black of violent revolution.

At the end of the tale Robin saves himself from joining in the full horror he has witnessed, withdrawing, as it were, into a daylight world of conscious, rational calculation. Thus he arrives at a condition of privileged orphanhood: he may rise in the world without the aid of his abased kinsman. Although his mocking laughter reveals his sympathy with the mob's violence – indeed, his long night's adventures are seen to have had this climactic encounter between debased authority and anarchic youth as their latent object – very little registers in the restricted boundaries of his conscious mind. This self-dissociation, or restraint of consciousness, which we find in many later characters (Dimmesdale, Holgrave, Coverdale, and Hilda, for example) is, as we shall see, not limited to Hawthorne. But it may be Hawthorne's way of not only dramatizing the thinness of personality, which he lamented in the men and women of his day, but of accounting for it as well. For in this tale we can discern the cost to personality of that self-restraint which a culture dedicated to self-reliant equality (an especially prominent theme in Jacksonian America) must impose if civic order is to be maintained.[8]

Just before this climax occurs, Robin's "friendly" guide, whose tone and bearing suggest a manlier version of the youth's own asks him, "May not one man have several voices . . . as well as two complexions?" (p. 226).[9] It is the burden of the tale that these several voices of Robin (who himself personifies the ambivalent qualities of "the popular mind") remain as divided from his "conscious researches" as is the red-black war paint which bifurcates the face of the devil-leader. For I believe the story turns on the fact that Robin and the crowd bear a reciprocal, though unacknowledged, relation to one another. This means more than is usually implied by a simple analogy between individual and national life. Just as the conscious values of the young country – decency, prudence, and innocent self-trust, as well as naive shrewdness and ambition – are mirrored in Robin's character and appearance so, in turn, are the hidden aspects of his nature externalized in the conspiratorial activity of the mysterious and threatening Others. Thus Robin, gazing at the horseman with drawn sword leading the procession, notes that " 'The double-faced fellow has his eye upon me,' . . . with an indefinite but an uncomfortable idea that he himself was to bear a part in the pageantry" (p. 228). Throughout the story, a complex linkage of symbol, image, and phrase gives us to understand that the violent act of rebellion on the town streets corresponds to the shadowy impulses of Robin's own unconscious mind.

As in many of his tales, Hawthorne here seems to utilize principles of Romantic historiography (and epistemology) in order to question some of the assumptions which this historiography embraced. For, as David Levin shows, the Romantic historians sought to embody the "spirit of the age" and to portray it through representative types whose qualities would reveal the national character which underlay national institutions. Furthermore, the American historians were committed to the belief that "history was the unfolding of a vast Providential plan" leading toward that democratic progress, of which America was the culmination.[10] So Hawthorne takes the Romantic faith in democratic progress and scrutinizes it through a representative type. But his hero is not a simple embodiment of those ideal moral qualities connoted by the phrase "virtue of the people"; rather, he is closer to their real nature, a democratic Everyman who has many voices, and many impulses within his breast. If, as Michael Colacurcio puts it, Hawthorne reduces the moral grandeur of the Revolution by showing the ordinariness of its provincial guilt,[11] he also shows us the severe limitations of that ideology of self-reliance which finds its proudest sanction in its revolutionary origins.

In effect, the ending presents us with the American future as Hawthorne seemed to feel it had become, its curiously empty sense of freedom epitomized in the aftermath of silence on the lonely street. But rather than offer a solution to the dramatic problem of Robin's dissociated identity, the ending reifies its terms. Robin's self-divided search for an inherited identity becomes the very definition of that identity. As in many of Hawthorne's tales, the moral asserted in the epilogue ("Perhaps, as you are a shrewd youth, you may rise in the world without the help of your kinsman, Major Molineux" [p. 231]) masks a darker, more discomforting insight. The point, I believe, is not that Robin may rise without the help of his kinsman, but that the ambition which shapes this desire to rise is predicated on a delusive denial of all that the past means, in terms of both individual consciousness and national endeavor.

At the climax, Hawthorne presents us with two contradictory acts which, taken together, make the assertion of the ending far more equivocal than it might otherwise seem. In bringing Robin face-to-face with his trembling kinsman, Hawthorne suggests that identity is not a thing to be found or given but to be made anew in each successive generation, dependent as it is upon a process of perception, of seeing oneself as a creature of history – one whose moral being is shaped in a dialectic with time and circumstance. However, the turn to which Hawthorne subjects this insight reveals the distinctive feature of Robin's American condition. It lies in his ability to blink away what he has just seen, to brace himself against the complex dynamics of human nature and human history and take refuge in their dream-like irrelevance to his own purposes. So Robin's gratuitous laughter, "the loudest there," is succeeded by Robin's self-protective withdrawal, as the frenzied uproar sweeps onward to the American future.

Although the story conceptualizes the psycho-dynamics of history in the poetics of dream language, the epilogue allows Robin to dismiss the affect of this metaphoric vocabulary in an "awakening" that reduces the rich interweave of image and symbol to a mere figure of speech, "Well, Robin, are you dreaming?" [p. 230]). Robin can rub his sleepy eyes and marvel at the nightmare from which he has just escaped. But to distance oneself from the

troubling truths of one's origins by stressing their oneiric uncertainty, as Robin's "guide" encourages him to do, is to diminish
the moral and imaginative texture of life in the present as well.
To ridicule the significance of one's primal relations is to evade
recognition of the power of their influence on one's present acts. It
is to rest in the delusive belief that good will and decent intentions
are means enough to re-invent society. So Robin's future success
is seen to depend upon his ability to maintain that self-division
which has characterized his night journey all along; not, as we
might conventionally expect, to overcome it by integrating its
warring components into a more profound understanding of what
patrimony means. What is most clear at the end of this tale is the
price that the self-sufficient ethos exacts from the American
character.

But if this were all that the ending asserted, the self-division I am
speaking of might seem a standard irony, intended as comment on
the popular image of the "American self." That is, the reader, if not
Robin, is finally brought face-to-face with glaring truth, as the narrator addresses us over the head of an imperceptive character.
However, although the plot depends upon Robin's misperceptions
and the narrative voice incorporates many shades of irony, I do
not believe it to be simple irony that most accurately characterizes
the effect of the epilogue. With the dream-like disappearance of
the mob, our sympathies, which were never far off, are drawn
back to Robin's new condition of isolated self-sufficiency.
Although, for the first time, Robin seems to recognize his "friend's"
share in the night's events, linking him with the other conspirators
(" 'You and my other friends' "), the guide is still just that – a
kindly, if skeptical figure through whom we, like Robin, are encouraged not to despair of an identity that, lonely as it is, leaves us
free from troubling aspects of our nature. Perhaps, like Robin, we
will do all right with no guide but the voice of rational consciousness. This final "perhaps" underscores the ambiguous new conditions of Robin's future. The note of equivocal hope it strikes is
one which we will find repeated in all the endings to be discussed.

The historian Edmund Morgan writes of the "genuine uneasi-
ness among the revolutionists about their own worthiness for the
role they had undertaken." Having cast off a corrupt monarchy,
their success depended entirely on their own virtue, and they were
not without intimidating fears of failure and isolation. By the time

Hawthorne wrote his tale, the Revolution was more than a generation old, but the fear of mob emotion and anarchic violence was
on the rise, not only in Jacksonian America but in those portions
of Europe with which Americans felt most akin.[12] The sense of an
identity at risk, an identity in which self-examination becomes
confounded with self-abandonment, with capitulation to forces
that threaten to destroy the decorum and order on which virtue
depends, becomes the motive for an ending that contravenes the
narrative logic of the tale. In ultimately siding with Robin's evasion, Hawthorne is revealing some of the powerful imperatives in
the American scene. But to make such a speculation about the
cultural context of this story we must be more precise as to how
the narrative both arouses and confounds thematic expectations.

Let us examine two complementary images that Hawthorne
utilizes to create an ironic perspective on an American archetype.
One of these can be found in *The Autobiography of Benjamin
Franklin* which, since its first publication, has served as prime
social myth.[13] In Part One, Franklin recreates for the reader the
experience of his entry into the city of Philadelphia as a young
man come to make his fortune. Arriving by water, he chooses,
prudently, to wait out the night in a creek above the city rather
than undertake a possibly futile search for it in the dark. Around
eight or nine o'clock on the following Sunday morning, he lands at
Market Street Wharf. Though tired and dirty from his long
journey, young Franklin is invigorated by the sights and sounds
of the waking town, his faith in his own possibilities reviving in
the fresh morning air. To stress the initiatory quality of this
entrance, he tells the reader that he has "been the more particular
in this Description of my Journey, and . . . of my first entry into the
City, that you may in your Mind compare such unlikely Beginnings with the Figure I have since then made."[14]

Forty years after the autobiography was first published, Hawthorne wrote the tale of another ambitious young man, another
pre-Revolutionary colonist as eager and canny as Franklin, who
arrives in Boston during the same historical period to make his
fortune. But unlike Franklin, Robin begins by seeking a promised
but unspecified patrimony from his royalist kinsman. Moreover,
Hawthorne's hero is not constructing his own story from the perspective of a prominent and successful old age. He is in the hands of
a narrator who sympathizes with him, but sees more deeply into his

nature and potential than he himself wishes to; a narrator whose
sense of moral complexity involves an ironic recognition of the
several voices and complexions to be found within the bounds of
an individual soul.

Robin's tone of confident good cheer makes him a sort of young
Ben Franklin who, for most of the tale, is the butt of his own conceit
that he is privileged to shape his own myth. In effect, the multi-
voiced irony of Hawthorne's narrative serves as comment
on the Franklinesque dream of a single-minded will. Unlike the
harmonies of Franklin's autobiography, the discord between
Robin's assumptions and the events surrounding him, which culminates in the "tuneless bray" of the procession, serves to underline
the pathos and shallow insularity of his self-delusion. In contrast to
Franklin, Robin's confident eye and bearing have no power (until
the end) to give significant shape to his surroundings. Scenes and
figures appear and disappear with a hallucinatory life of their own.
This sense of dislocation in a world of undecipherable and confus-
ing meanings is established at the outset with Robin's night arrival
in the dark, silent town – a lone passenger, ferried across a nameless river by a silent, staring ferryman. The mood is one of descent
to an underworld, a hellish wilderness; the river might be the Styx,
whose name connects it with the Greek word for hateful and
gloomy.

Robin's quest for his kinsman suggests the initiatory pattern of
folk and fairy tale – the youth without name or fortune who
arrives at a seat of power, often in disguise, to claim his rightful
inheritance and thus establish his identity. In these tales we often
respond to a sense of order re-established through generational passage, which allays worries that are at once social and individual.[15]
But unlike these traditional quest figures, whose tasks and purposes
are clearly defined, Robin's relation to his goal is confused from
the outset. His arrival is a gamble, based on the recollection of a
vague promise offered by a cousin he hasn't seen for years. He
doesn't know where this man dwells, what he now looks like, or
even what role he plays in the town. At the beginning of the
tale the narrator tells us that Robin is only one of the youth's
several names. (What the others may be, of course, remains unrevealed to the end.) Moreover, in all his inquiries for the kinsman
he claims to be seeking, Robin never identifies himself by any
surname, although since his father and the Major are sons of

brothers, it is clear that this would have to be Molineux. The ambiguity with which both Robin and the narrator surround his name – a name, like an inheritance, that would normally link past with future – is only one of the several devices by which Hawthorne dramatizes the conflicted aspirations of the young nation which, like an adolescent, believes its identity to be entirely in its own keeping, even as it seeks both the blessing and destruction of paternal authority.[16]

Until the last, each approach of a likely elder or guide ends in some form of betrayal or humiliation for Robin. Desire turns to shame, bravado to supplication. And after each encounter his suppressed anger bursts forth in fantasies of mock violence. In a series of quasi-surreal images, the narrator evokes the warring impulses of a spirit steeped in Franklinesque virtues of self-restraint and consciously wedded to their promise of success. Like the young Ben Franklin, Robin never despairs, is always shrewd, confident, and optimistic. But the narrative eye illumines the narrow boundaries of this pragmatic consciousness, around and beneath which lies the primitive horror of the confrontation Robin has been both seeking and avoiding all night long. What we are led to see at the climax of Robin's circuitous journey is not a sanctified image of the well-pruned national tree, not the calculus of a future of order and abundance toward which Franklin's moral accounting would urge us, but the face of rebellion as primal violence and terror; that parricidal aggression which is part of man's inherent nature and mocks Robin's cheerful eighteenth-century faith in the rational will. This is the dark side of Franklin's social myth of economic opportunity and ethical decency. Hawthorne seems to be asking here: if human nature cannot remake itself in America, how can it make an ideal America?

The story is so dazzling in its dramatic rendering of psychological complexity, in its conflation of social myth and psychic archetype, that it is easy to miss noticing the curious and all-important role of the narrator. As Richard Poirier has pointed out, it is the narrator who judges and condemns the action to which young Robin joins his guilty laughter.[17] While the fallen father-king, the old Major, trembling in the throes of shame and humiliation, stares at Robin, the narrative voice, which until now has maintained a cool, disinterested tone, speaks out in force. Like a voice which might have emanated from the Major himself, it condemns the rebellious mob which has overturned the king's agent with this mock-castration for "trampling all on an old man's heart." Robin, holding fast to his post to avoid being caught up in the "living stream," barely holding, as it were, to the narrow path of his rational will, may thus be seen to be heeding the narrator's words. Considering Robin's subsequent actions, the voice which addresses the reader may equally be conceived as one of several in Robin's own head. And it is a voice surely intended to be believed, for the phrase underscores the moral meaning implicit in Hawthorne's aesthetic strategy. In making Robin and the crowd reciprocal parts of one another, Hawthorne is not utilizing an allegorical device merely to facilitate psychological expression. Rather, I believe, he is dramatizing one aspect of the complex interrelation between individual and community which underlies his concern with the significance of history.

In meeting the eyes of his humiliated kinsman, Robin is brought to the edge of a terrifying self-recognition. The meaning toward which all his night's inquiries have been tending now manifests itself in the train of wild figures and fantastic shapes, "as if a dream had broken forth from some feverish brain" (p. 228). So, in the wake of the universal hum, he stares at the old man as his knees shake and his hair bristles in a classic "mixture of pity and terror." But a moment later Robin is seized by a "bewildering excitement." What is stressed in this cruel ritual is its mutual denigration of subject and object. Just as Major Molineux has been reduced to a horrifying abstraction in the tar and feather smearing, so that emblem of democratic sanctity, "the people" has been transmogrified into an abandoned mob dependent upon a brutal leader. The laughter of the crowd, to which Robin joins his voice ("the loudest there"), serves as a momentary compromise with his violent hostility, allowing him to deflect rather than act upon it. But just as surely as it bespeaks further discord, it signals the eclipse of that moral feeling bred from a respect for the ineluctable dignity of others, upon which genuine individualism depends. Ultimately, the laughter raises the disquieting (and still unanswered) question of what the grounds of American identity actually are. From what and from whom shall this new American self take its measure?

Robin's search for a patrimony, hedged with images of violence and death – his desire to inherit even as he wants to overthrow and destroy – is a common enough adolescent paradox, as Simon Lesser pointed out long ago.[18] But in this tale the ambivalence is neither resolved through the protagonist's deeper insight into the nature of the contradictions (as many critics who follow this pure Oedipal reading often assume), nor, most significantly, does Robin suffer the full cost of his choice of an orphaned state. Having seen his kinsman tarred and feathered he acknowledges that his kinsman will no longer wish to see him (nor, we note, be able to help him). But he, and we, are assured that shrewd Robin will, no doubt, survive without him. Leaving innocence behind, Robin is guided toward that neutral territory of rising hopes.

If to recognize one's own chaotic impulses entails giving oneself to the brutalities of a frenzied mob, it is no wonder that prudence as well as sanity dictate turning away from the full horror of such knowledge. But it is Hawthorne who has established these extreme either/or terms in which the issues are conceived. From "Young Goodman Brown" to *The Marble Faun*, his last completed work, Hawthorne's plots regularly seem to dictate either a frightening loss of self in the unchartered realms of human emotion (often associated with a mob), or a withdrawal from conflict which leaves its subjects socially and spiritually diminished.

The question that interests me here is not why this phenomenon should persist in Hawthorne's work, for that would inevitably lead toward a biographical cul-de-sac; but why, in differing modes, this Hobson's choice between self-suppression on the one hand and self-annihilation on the other, recurs in so many diverse American writers. And I believe this story offers a clue. Robin provides us with a graphic image of the problematic of American individualism. His self-sufficiency is not unique but representative; his individuality not that of one among many social possibilities (as we might see it portrayed in European novels and tales) but a prototype of the American character. Thus, to acknowledge fully his own worst nature would be tantamount to denying that dream of a rising America prefigured in his new-found self-reliance. Yehoshua Arieli has pointed out that the term "individualism," which in the Old World was almost synonymous with selfishness, social anarchy, and individual self-assertion, connoted in America self-determination, moral freedom, the rule of liberty, and the dignity of man. It came to represent the highest and final stage of human progress.[19] So

Hawthorne, for all his skepticism about the dark side of American autonomy, can find no alternative to it but a self-restraint amounting to self-repression, if the ambition to which autonomy is allied is to maintain its cultural primacy.

Tocqueville, observing the country just at the time this tale was published, thought that the democratic obsession with equality might ultimately lead to the dissolution of democracy itself. Hawthorne here seems to be examining just this potential at the heart of American revolutionary aspiration. But having led us to the abyss, as it were, he allows the tragic force of these questions to dissipate under more pragmatic considerations of survival. Robin clings to his post; the procession sweeps on without him; the street returns to silence and emptiness. As the nightmare dissolves, the narrative voice resolves into that of Robin's skeptical but kindly guide. With the invitation to remain in town to rise "without the help . . . of Major Molineux," the possibility that Robin will be able to shape his own myth, write his own story, is reopened; the bold irony that brought the American dream of moral and economic self-sufficiency face-to-face with the realities of human nature subsides.

By repressing the chaos of being beneath a shrewd Yankee conscience, Robin is confirmed in the narrow Franklinesque character of his conscious self. The night has indeed been an initiation. For contrast, one thinks of Conrad's famous dictum, spoken by Stein in *Lord Jim*: "to the destructive element submit yourself; and with the exertions of your hands and feet in the water make the deep, deep sea keep you up."[20] Such a concept of survival would involve a deeper recognition of self and circumstance than Hawthorne allows even his most psychologically acute characters to register.

Two themes, then, are established in this tale of protonational identity. One is the will to revolutionary violence toward the father-nation and its primal authority; the other is the calculated optimism of the youth who claims to seek only what is owed him, what is just, decent, and fair. How to bring these two conflicting views into accommodation to each other, either in terms of *realpolitik* or in terms of tragic insight, might be conceived as the central problem of the story. But recognition is precisely what is shrouded in the equivocation of the ending. Neither the moral cost of anarchic energies released, nor the truly frightening resultant reality of self-definition without guidance is acknowledged. A guide, in fact, is provided, the "friendly" voice in Robin's own ear. It is as if Ben Franklin himself were standing beside Robin. The complex present is denied while the lost community of Robin's boyhood, the colonial childhood of the nation, is transmuted into the equivocal promise of a rising future. On the brink of the unknown, Franklin's voice soothes us. Though our writers are often grouped into convenient figures of darkness and light (like the fair and dark ladies of melodrama), this division fails, I believe, to do full justice to the genuine intertwining of attitudes and images which emerges in these works.

Bleak Dreams: Restriction and Aspiration in *The Scarlet Letter*

ON A FIELD SABLE, THE LETTER A GULES

Hawthorne's tale of "human frailty and sorrow" closes with this dark epitaph drawn from the tombstone that marks the lovers' double grave. The words refer to an heraldic inscription whose symbolic conjunction of red and black can be traced through the entire novel, reminding us of the power, destructive force, and inevitable limitations of human passion.[1] The image of the tombstone itself harks back to the narrator's opening comment that "The founders of a new colony, whatever Utopia of virtue and happiness they might originally project" must of necessity allot "a portion of the virgin soil" to cemetery and prison.[2] Thus the shape of the narrative metaphorically reinforces the awareness felt throughout the tale of crime and death as encircling conditions of human life. This awareness would seem to underscore the futility of those visionary ambitions to which the passions of all the protagonists, but especially Hester's, are allied.

The theme of the anarchic energies and dangers of human passion links *The Scarlet Letter* to Hawthorne's earlier story, "My Kinsman, Major Molineux." (Even the red-black motif is anticipated in the warpaint of the devil leader in the latter.) However, in *The Scarlet Letter* the violence is internalized and largely self-inflicted, the rebellion generated by an act of love, not hate. Yet nothing in American literature up to this point provides as bleak a prognosis for happiness in the New World as that which Hawthorne gives us in this anatomy of the human soul. For though *The Scarlet Letter* is set in the historical past, it seems to me to be a profoundly contemporaneous work. In translating the Calvinist preoccupation with the fallen condition of human existence into a species of psychological drama, Hawthorne utilizes the structure and ideology of the Puritan community to explore a problematic cultural inheritance whose issue is of primary concern to his own historical period. While each of the major characters in the novel is blighted, as it were, by the consequence of a type of the Fall – a given spontaneous act which united Hester and Arthur in a forbidden love – their suffering is intensified by that mutual isolation which in Hawthorne's day could already be recognized as the dark twin of self-reliant individualism.

Each of the characters is engrossed in a self-preoccupation so acute that for seven years they are barely aware of one another's presence. Locked in their several versions of isolate autonomy, each acts as sole judge and witness to the moral meaning of his or her own acts. Until the end, none allows the touch of affection, compassion or the pressure of another's need to pierce their solitude. This mutual blindness is complemented by a self-suppression severe enough to make each the chief violator of his or her own humanity.[3] Denied the emotional and spiritual nourishment of genuine human community, the three adult protagonists waste into shadow, becoming ghosts of the men and women they might once have been. Red – the color of passion, liberty, and spontaneous life – is visualized on the tombstone escutcheon at the close as a persistent but tiny point of light, glowing dimly, even "gloomier than the shadow" which surrounds it.

Yet just before this final image Hawthorne has given us a view of Hester looking into the future, her visionary hopes undimmed by what she has suffered. Chastened but apparently undaunted, she acknowledges that although she herself can no longer hope to be the prophetess of a new truth, as once she had, she looks forward to that "brighter period . . . [when] in Heaven's own time, a new truth would be revealed, in order to establish the whole relation between man and woman on a surer ground of mutual happiness" (p. 168). But the dream that Hester clings to is tantamount to the transformation of humanity itself. It seeks to transcend the limitations, not only of Puritan Boston or the society of Hawthorne's own day, but those which any social order must impose if it is to provide stability for human nature as it is, rather than as we may wish it to be.

Hester's dream is a revision of the theme of her forest injunction to Dimmesdale to be "up, and away," to begin life over again. Fittingly, her seven years as an outcast reach their climax in the actual wilderness because it has been her increasing ambition, through the course of the story, to deny those internal as well as external boundaries which would subvert her claim to an ideal identity. What this penultimate paragraph does is to reshape Hester's dream of a new life with Arthur by projecting it into the future and expanding it to encompass all men and women. Her "A," which once provoked scorn and bitterness, now commingles awe, reverence, and sorrow in those around her. But for all the alteration in its meaning, it remains a mask – an outline or abstraction of human identity that substitutes for true individuality, absorbing the remainder of Hester's personal, spontaneous life into itself. In this penultimate paragraph, her individual social rebellion is recast; in retrospect it becomes a process of initiation into a new and representative form of consciousness whose goal, "the perfection of the whole society," mirrors the original Puritan corporate ideal (a community of saints) which it effectively replaces.[4]

At the close, then, we see Hester, shorn of her rich European heritage, assuming the burden of a self that she and the town have created between them. An archetypal outsider and dreamer, counselor to women, living for no private pleasures or selfish ends, she is at once exalted and impoverished. Like the nation whose identity she now seems to prefigure, she is rooted nowhere. While she dreams of future social perfection, she narrows the circumstances of her daily life to those of an ascetic or saint. Her return to America and resumption of her badge may be conceived as an act that joins her to the sorrows of human history, but Hester still yearns for the liberating moment when history will be made anew.[5]

Taken together with the cemetery imagery in the last lines of the story, these two final paragraphs are akin to a pictorial diptych. In one panel Hester dreams of the transcendent American future; in the other the tombstone is a stark reminder of the limits of human destiny. But does Hester herself ever acknowledge the discrepancy between these two perspectives? Does she ever achieve a self-recognition parallel to Dimmesdale's experience on the scaffold? In place of such a recognition which must, as it is with Dimmesdale, be individual and personal before it can have communal issue, Hester resumes her badge and dissolves her private personality in what Sacvan Bercovitch has called "prophetic solace."[6] Hester's badge, as I have indicated above, would seem an alternative to self-recognition, not an expression of it.

At the end of the book, Hester's is the dominant voice. It is her view of the future that prevails. On the scaffold she had cried to Arthur: "Thou lookest far into eternity with those bright dying eyes! Then tell me what thou seest?" (p. 181). But Arthur can only answer her in the traditional rhetoric of Christian dogma. His perception of experience is bound to a theologically ordained interpretation of events. All he can be sure of is that they are sinners in God's eyes. It is only Hester who has the imaginative freedom to envision experience anew. And, at the last, Hawthorne protects the hope to which this freedom is bound. For surely the view we have of Hester's last days would be different if she fully acknowledged the limitations of the human condition in less ambiguous terms than those in which Hawthorne envelops her thoughts. Describing her return to America, he tells us that "here was yet to be the scene of her penitence" (p. 185). And while she absents herself from the active role of "apostle of the coming revelation," she dreams that such a prophetess as she might have been will one day arise (p. 186). Hester's vision of a new truth that will change the whole relation between men and women seems to involve the idea that her penitential vigil will one day be rewarded by a spiritual purification that will make such an exercise unnecessary. It is no wonder that the ambiguities in these phrases, as well as the feminist sentiment which pervades them, have contributed to so many diverse readings of the novel and evaluations of Hawthorne's ultimate intention.

And, paradoxically, it is the many conflicting readings, which extend from Hawthorne's day to ours – with Hester either repentent or recalcitrant, romantically liberated or theologically redeemed – that suggest the work's continuing dramatic relevance to our culture's most hallowed themes. For though the popularity of the tale doubtless lies in the perennial fascination of tragically thwarted love, its power just as surely derives from the tension of values at its heart, where a rigid autarchic idealism struggles with the longing for a social order that is humane, compassionate and grounded in an ethic of reciprocal moral responsibility.

Yet, more often than not, critical opinion, faced with the contradictory pattern of the ending, has managed to evade its equivocations, either by ignoring them and taking Dimmesdale's scaffold scene for the book's true end, or by reducing them to a single assertion about Hawthorne's intention.[7] My own view owes much to two critics who have not tried to simplify the book's disjunctive qualities. Quentin Anderson stresses Hawthorne's commitment to a concept of community that is the opposite of Hester's visionary longings – not an abstract futuristic Utopia, but a more authentic present, based on the sense that life is "rootedly reciprocal," that we find our meaning and value only through our relations with others. But for Professor Anderson, Hawthorne's ending represents his failure to carry through his fight with his own age. By suggesting that "what has distorted Hester Prynne has in some measure made her a prophetess . . . Hawthorne . . . has responded to his age . . . [by] cobbling up a religion of his own."[8]

Yt the point to be stressed here is that this "religion" seems not at all an afterthought. I believe, rather, Hawthorne is resurrecting a version of the tarnished ideology that Hester has embodied all along, and in so doing he reaffirms its continuing hold on the American imagination. What has distorted her has indeed made her a prophetess. The tensions in Hester's character provide both a critique and an exemplum of that mix of values which has issued in American idealism. Had Hawthorne allowed her the self-recognition which he withholds, she would surely be a more humanly tragic figure; but she would relinquish that emblematic status which in large measure has been responsible for her survival.

Hester's final days are conceived in a spirit that brings her close to what Sacvan Bercovitch has defined as "representative heroism." Like her counterparts in the popular historical romances of the period, Hester, rebel and outcast, is discovered to be the "representative American woman . . . the spirit incarnate of democracy, liberty and progress."[9] However, as Professor Bercovitch also notes, Hawthorne enmeshes his heroine in so much historical complexity that the prophetic stance which characterizes her role is ultimately a rather shaky affair.

In fact, it is this complexity which suggests that Hawthorne, more intensely perhaps than any other writer discussed in this book, contained, in Lionel Trilling's phrase, a large part of his culture's "yes and no" within himself; that for him – especially on the evidence of his later work – the tension of this dialectic was increasingly irresolvable.[10]

From the book's outset, Hawthorne pits Hester's claim to moral autonomy against that of the equally autocratic Puritan town. There is an ironic kinship underlying the counterpoint between

31

these two forces. In the name of freedom of conscience and purity of intent, each has separated itself from Old World ties. Each presents an image of singular purpose set against the background of the New World wilderness – a condition which not only reinforces the spiritual and moral realities that each must face alone but also evokes the hope of rebirth and renewal that each cherishes. Hester, standing on the scaffold before the grim Puritan crowd, her three-month infant crying in her arms, is bounded by a solitude which, paradoxically, makes her the focus of all eyes. Asserting the imperative of her own conscience against the dictates of the Puritan authorities, she refuses to break her silence and betray the name of her lover to the magistrates. The tiny Puritan settlement believes that it too has an absolute responsibility to assert and enforce God's truth, that its errand in the New World is to serve as spiritual beacon to the world across the sea – in Winthrop's words, the "eyes of all people are upon us." The spiritual Utopia that the settlers are building in America will be the model for the redemption of all mankind.[11]

In putting Europe behind her, Hester has shared the same fervor for new beginnings that motivated the ocean crossing of the dissenting Puritans. But her independent moral stance, coupled with her assertive sexuality, presents a classic antithesis to the restrictive, patriarchal theocracy represented by her Puritan judges. If Hester has wandered into the book from the nineteenth century, her anachronistic posture only underscores Hawthorne's historicizing intent. Blending elements of Emersonian individualism with those of its seventeenth-century antinomian prototype, Hawthorne dramatizes the dialectical persistence of an historical ideal.

Hester, drawn to a dynamic principle of self-shaping – the American who can be and do whatever he chooses, give up one name and make another "and a high one" – voices a latter-day optimistic vision of social regeneration that necessarily conflicts with the more ancient and severe construction of human nature embodied in her lover, Dimmesdale, and upheld by the Puritan elders. As we first see her, with her newborn child sheltered on her breast and her unremitting protection of the name of the child's father, she suggests that generosity of feeling and nurturing passion out of which life might germinate anew. But it is the burden of the book to dramatize the tragic waste which ensues from the misdirection of such resources of body and heart, then as now, and not solely for Hester but for the community to which she is dialectically bound.

From the moment that Hester steps forth from the prison door, shaking off the beadle's hand, the stigma of her crime on her breast has the ironic effect of freeing the crowd watching her from any compunction to identify with her. By isolating and objectifying Hester, turning her into a text on sin "in all its branches," the community rejects the possibility that her suffering has any personal meaning for it. In taking the letter for the spirit, the Puritans have perversely driven her into a wilderness of false freedom, liberating her and themselves from the mutual necessity for compassion and sympathy. So Hester, "giving up her individuality" (p. 59), returns in kind what she gets from the town. Instead of charitable feelings there are only charitable acts. Her apparent humility masks an unremitting pride, behind which she projects her sin everywhere, seeing in the faces of the passing townspeople nothing but their complicity in crime. Though she recognizes this to be a futile exercise, she cannot help herself. For though the town surely has its quota of secret sinners, Hester is no more able to conceive of her fellow colonists as individuals than they can see her as one. Even when their attitude softens and they begin to reinterpret her "A" as Able, she remains imprisoned in her initial view of them. Any effort to greet or accost her she rebuffs by laying "a finger on the scarlet letter" and passing on (p. 117).

In mistaking this silent pride for humility and her charitable deeds for a change of heart, the Puritans unwittingly prove the truth of their own theological doctrine that good works are not enough. Conversely, their misperception also reveals the antinomian dangers inherent in their doctrine. For since we cannot judge by acts alone, what is to prevent us from finding ourselves in the wilderness with Hester, proclaiming the sanctity of our motives against a world similarly inclined?

Hawthorne's antidote for this, the age-old one of our moral relation to others, takes on particular urgency in the climate of self-preoccupation and ensuing isolation which is the book's normative atmosphere, and which he seems to suggest was the occupational hazard and legacy of Puritanism.[12] As a web of vital obligations and reciprocal sympathies, the legendary Puritan community hardly exists. All we see of its individual members is a

conclave of magistrates and elders who, for all their putative saint-
liness, are unable to comprehend the emotional needs of the mother
and child whose lives are under their care. Apart from this one
scene, the community is depicted only as a generalized crowd, with
an emphasis on its women whose vindictive temper is replicated in
their stone-throwing children, who repeatedly attack little Pearl.
It is through the change in attitude of these women, who dominate
both the opening scaffold scene and the close of the book, as they
seek out Hester's counsel, that Hawthorne indicates both the drift
of historical process and the outline of what is missing here – those
lineaments of a genuine community in which women would share
with, and not be opposed to or isolated from, men. But within this
proto-American settlement, which, as we have noted, Hawthorne's
nineteenth-century audience had mythologized as the source of
both its liberties and prophetic destiny,[13] compassion, mercy, and
a decent regard for the humanity of others – surely primary
characteristics of any "civilized" settlement, much less one with
utopian aspirations – are shown to be profoundly difficult human
achievements.

Nor, as he makes clear, have Hawthorne's nineteenth-century
readers achieved any better normative relations than the characters within his story. For to be oneself in a wilderness of mental
solitude, whether harshly ostracized or genteelly ridiculed, is seen
to be a contradiction in terms. It is to lose one's attachment to the
necessary grounds of identity. So behind her barricade of silence
Hester constructs grandiose fantasies of a radically anarchic freedom which, were it known, would be considered by the Puritan
establishment a far graver crime than that for which she wears the
letter. But for Hawthorne, the gravest danger in her speculations
is their tendency to dehumanize her by de-sexualizing her nature;
to offer a specious compensation for her loss of objects on which
to lavish the warmth and passion of her feelings. Only a loving
reciprocity with another can provide the antidote to the frustra-
tion and violence presaged in her thoughts. By shunning and
humiliating her, the town has turned the initial wildness and spontaneity of her nature (symbolized by her fantastic embroidery of
the "A") into what Hawthorne presents as the contorting features
of a radical feminist ideology. For it is surely the feminism of his
own day that he has in mind in his bemusement with Hester's
dreams of tearing down the whole system of society, modifying

"the nature of the opposite sex," and then finally of changing woman's nature so that she can properly take advantage of all these changes once in place. What is lost, says Hawthorne (perhaps in a manifestation of his own idealism), is that "ethereal essence" in which a woman "has her truest life" (p. 120).

To a modern ear, the ironies in this account of Hester's thoughts tend to be weakened by the excessive sentimentality of phrases like the last two quoted above. It may therefore be tempting to follow the line of one critic who has claimed that Hawthorne created a vivid transcendental heroine only to censure her because he was uncomfortable with his own radical impulses.[14] But to do so would be to narrow severely one's understanding of what Hester experiences and why. Hawthorne goes to great lengths to make the elements of her character – her beauty, passion, strength and independent spirit – appealing and convincing. But the novelistic qualities of his work are nowhere more in evidence than when he suggests that her idealism and courage, while never deserting her, take their direction from the circumstances of her life. Thus, while we sympathize with the extremity of her thoughts (else we as an audience would be in the same position toward her as is the town), we are always aware of the desperation they reflect, as well as of their human improbability. In time, Hester's idealism hardens into that of the prisoner and outcast. This is the source of both her power and pathos. Though rebellion, Hawthorne seems to say, is part of the germ of her being, it has blossomed into a false freedom, as distorting to her nature as Dimmesdale's tortures are to his. So in the one idyllic passage in the book, when it seems that the mutual love Hester has longed for may be finally within her grasp, Hawthorne reminds us of the inadequacy of her vision to the psychology of human needs. Neither Dimmesdale nor, more importantly, Pearl could thrive in the freedom of the forest as Hester envisions it. What for her is natural law is for Dimmesdale an anarchy of impulse and for Pearl only a moment of play – a freedom of fantasy dependent upon the safety of her mother's familiar presence.

Ultimately, it is Pearl, as Hester herself says in her plea to the magistrates, "who keeps me here in life" (p. 83); that is, who reminds her of both the good and evil in her own nature. For Pearl, mingling psychological with allegorical strains of truth, both mirrors Hester's nature ("the scarlet letter endowed with

35

life!") and reveals the limitations of Hester's self-reliant morality. Thus, in the forest, Pearl insists that her mother replace the familiar "A" on her breast and so re-affirm the contours of their mutually familiar world – a response which attests to Pearl's need for a consistent moral structure founded on a more resilient truth than the vagaries of individual impulse can provide.

In looking for her own reflection in Pearl's dark pupils, Hester discerns a shadow of what she thinks of as the evil that had existed within herself and may now, she fears, be divined in Pearl. She imagines that she sees a fiend-like face, "full of smiling malice, yet bearing the semblance of features that she had known full well . . ." (p. 72). She attributes this to the work of an evil spirit who possesses the child; but it is Hester's own distorted features that are mirrored in her child's eyes. And when she puts the question, "Child, what art thou?" (p. 72), Pearl rightly answers, "It is thou that must tell me!" (p. 73). Yet as long as Hester remains imprisoned by the bitter distortions of her spirit, Pearl will search in vain for the clues to her own identity. What she demands as she grows is an image of self derived from two parents; and it is the public acknowledgment of this truth, in all its social as well as personal ramifications, toward which she goads Arthur and Hester.

Through her uncanny intuitions and imperious demands Pearl becomes the destabilizing agent in her parents' frozen existence. As a living hieroglyphic of their relation, her nature reflects the complex chain of emotion and responsibility which their unpremeditated impulse engendered. Her providential mission to them both culminates on the scaffold when she kisses Dimmesdale in broad daylight. The current of sympathy between individuals, which Dimmesdale first felt during his midnight vigil as he held Pearl's warm hand, completes itself in this kiss which serves as a pledge that Pearl would not "forever do battle with the world, but be a woman in it" (p. 181). Again, it is a gesture which emphasizes what has been absent all along – reminding us that at the core of community lies the redemptive power of human love.

For although the narrative of *The Scarlet Letter* turns on the inner dynamics of the four major characters, to sever these from the meaning of community is to ignore the principle by which Hawthorne evaluates the moral drama of individual lives. As each character is necessarily implicated in the inner life of the others, so the pattern created by these four interlinked souls offers a magnified image of the primal passions out of which community is formed. As Chillingworth declares in his first interview with Hester: "I find here a woman, a man, a child, amongst whom and myself there exist the closest ligaments. No matter whether of love or hate; no matter whether of right or wrong" (p. 58). Indeed, it is the drama of these primal passions gone awry, their energies turned against themselves, which enforces a sense of the terrible vulnerability of human identity to self-destruction when institutions and individuals fail each other. The depth of feeling which binds together Arthur, Hester, and Pearl, and which can only be revealed in the final scaffold scene, bespeaks a blindness in American social reality to the forms necessary to support and sustain authentic human relations. As Hawthorne depicts it, American communal life, in both its seventeenth- and nineteenth-century versions, has failed to generate those institutionalized sanctions of charity, generosity, or forgiveness which would testify to a positive recognition of the value of the individual soul.

It is this human failure which I take to be the central indictment of the novel – the loss of a normative historical community that is quite the opposite of the visionary ideal to which Hester dedicates herself at the end. Although this novel, like the others to be discussed, establishes a dichotomy between reality and vision, Hawthorne, unlike the other novelists, suggests that his idealist's stance is intimately connected to the loss. Hester's idealism hardens with time as a compensation for her exclusion from human society. Though she claims an *a priori* certainty in her views, Hawthorne does not seem to share this belief, since he shows their development within the history of her own experience.

If Hester's radical ideology is the misguided effect of her social isolation, equally misguided is Arthur's hope of achieving moral perfection through a punitive self-scrutiny that utterly divides and disguises him from the community he seeks to lead. Though Arthur is egoistically zealous to live up to ideals which his parishioners imagine they see in his person, his isolation is more monotonously severe than Hester's – his only human attachment the probing, vengeful physician whose "healing" frets Arthur to near madness. Whether we read Chillingworth as Christian devil or Freudian superego, the effect is the same. Arthur cannot recognize the nature of his worst enemy because he does not see that his project of self-torment (demonized in Chillingworth) is a strategy for denying, by disguising from himself, his common humanity with others. To free himself he must, as he finally does, acknowledge first to himself and then publicly his own human limitations. His self-torments are futile because they are based on the hope of achieving a private redemption without reference to his ties to Hester and Pearl. The obsessive cycle of guilt, remorse, and self-punishment that he pursues not only breeds hypocrisy and increases despair, but also, in its rigid defensiveness against the acknowledgment of his human needs and desires, is as stubbornly prideful as the charitable acts which mask Hester's hatred of the town. While Hester, in her isolation, projects her sin onto every face she passes, Arthur, driven to seek evidence of a self whose reality he can no longer feel, sees his guilty nature enlarged to the proportions of a fiery "A" spread out against the sky.

It is the central irony of Dimmesdale's condition that the pain which he cannot openly express is the source of the increasing effectiveness of his sermons. His capacity to affect his parishioners with the emotional undertones of his torment, and so deepen their response to his words, increases as his own secret sufferings advance. Dimmesdale's sermons are the equivalent of Hester's needlework; they are the art into which he pours his buried emotions. Like the hand he invariably holds to his chest, they both mask and assert the complex depths of their creator's secret identity. The implication would seem to be that Dimmesdale's capacity for authentic moral leadership, had he the strength and courage to exercise it in genuine communion with his parishioners (and they to accept it), would be great indeed. It is not a sinless or perfectly joyful community that Hawthorne predicates as a possibility in the major portion of the book, but a more honest, responsive, and authentically charitable one.

It is therefore crucial to the purport of the tale that Chillingworth's words to Hester confirm a truth of both their lives: "I pity thee, for the good that has been wasted in thy nature" (p. 125). As this is true for Hester, it is even more so for her former husband. For Chillingworth, more than any of them, has been his own worst enemy. Though, in a perversion of Calvinist theology, he pleads a determinism that absolves him of all personal responsibility, his commitment to villainy has actually been undertaken out of the freest, least conditioned set of circumstances in the book. As an outsider to the community, a scholar of some renown, he might have left as anonymously as he came, without any social stigma upon him. Having most freely chosen to remain and associate himself with the town, the evil to which he gives himself is as complete as his ability to choose it. As an exemplar of the rationalized cruelty and sadism to which the liberated will can descend, he turns out to be Hawthorne's best answer to the value of social restriction and the conditioned existence.

One of the most significant themes adumbrated in Alexis de Tocqueville's study of Jacksonian America is formulated as the problem of community in democratic society. Observing the environment of Hawthorne's day, Tocqueville repeatedly noted the lack of awareness of a genuine public sphere. Each man seemed to live apart, "centered in himself." What was lacking were those organic associations and institutions which foster "the reciprocal influence of men upon one another . . . The heart is enlarged and the human mind developed only by these influences [which] are almost null in democratic countries."[15] Whether or not this view has merit as a generalization about democracy, as an account of the ethos of Jacksonian America (as well as a prophecy of America's future), one can find resonant support for it in the work of our major contemporaneous authors. Melville, Emerson, Thoreau, Cooper might each be adduced, but Hawthorne, with his interest in the etiology as well as the psychology of American democratic idealism, gives us, perhaps, the most detailed evidence for its validity.

Indeed, it is from just this point that he seems to start in shaping his town and defining the relationships that characterize it. For though his rendering of the historical Puritan colony – its hierarchy, exclusivity, and homogeneity – is consistent with the facts of modern scholarship, Hawthorne's Boston is structured to emphasize those disabling qualities in American society that seem endemic, if not to democracy at large, then at least to our historical version of it.

When we turn from the major characters to the surrounding community, we note that both common people and magistrates share a tendency toward abstract conceptualization. While the crowd is governed by a set of simplified, schematic moral perceptions and easily swayed by fear, envy, and adulation, the elders, in their sense of total responsibility for the welfare of their constituents, are given to coldly rational judgments that deny the link between emotional and moral life. Though Hawthorne credits the seriousness of their effort to envision history as a drama which gives the utmost dignity to individual choice and act, their lack of compassion ultimately narrows the moral life to a set of bitter, retributive judgments. By keeping his outline faithful to the corporate ideal which underlay Puritan social structure, Hawthorne is able to suggest much about mass response and representative power in democratic culture. By the same token, the crowd's reverence for Dimmesdale and shunning of Hester, while no doubt consistent with the forms of Puritan behavior, encourages a metonymic reading. The situation of these tormented souls can be seen as representative of the pain to which the reification and alienation of others – particularly acute in a competitive, free-market society – inevitably leads.

Indeed, the book seems designed to reinforce the notion that simplified abstractions of any kind have no epistemological merit. For although the world of *The Scarlet Letter* appears to be structured by a set of contrasting principles, each defined in terms of its "other," these oppositions, once probed, unfold to reveal dynamic interconnections that multiply moral perspectives and meanings. The story begins with the all-inclusive contrast between human idealism (the New World Jerusalem envisaged by the Puritans) and man's fallen nature (the Boston prison and cemetery). But the multiple oppositions which immediately follow – old age, youth; authority, rebellion; moral responsibility, sexual passion; maternity, paternity; inward feeling, outward show; black magic, white magic; past, future; community of the book, community of its readers; America, Europe; forest, town – lead us neither toward a rigid, allegorical definition of an ideal state, nor toward the possibility of a simple moral choice between values. Our view is decidedly not that of the Puritan "popular mind." Rather, we discover ourselves to be in a bewildering labyrinth of interrelations which undermines the apparent stability of these dichotomies.

The Boston theocracy, with its sense of spiritual mission, is also the scene of Hester's passionate love, of Chillingworth's closest human ties, and of Dimmesdale's self-torment and ultimate atonement. It is the heaven and hell of the book. Yet it is also a conventional social landscape where none of these truths is evident to the townspeople, where all emotion is hidden or disguised. The moral strictures of the Puritan elders blind them to truths of feeling, while their pleasure in color and ornament at home consorts oddly with their dour public appearance. Out of the house of the righteous and responsible Governor Bellingham peeps his sister, Mistress Hibbins, who claims to be on intimate terms with the devil. Roger Chillingworth, European scholar and physician, enters the story accompanied by an Indian savage. He has been learning to mingle the arts of the forest with the heritage of medieval learning. Chillingworth himself is at once penitent toward Hester, acknowledging the wrong he did her in drawing her into an unlikely marriage, and vengeful toward Dimmesdale who, nevertheless, wronged him. He serves as goad to Dimmesdale's conscience and in the process destroys his own soul. Hester is both passionate in her attachment to Arthur and the indirect cause of his debility and death as she allows Chillingworth to prey on him unrevealed for seven years. Under any conditions, Dimmesdale's virtues – his capacity for intense self-scrutiny and painful self-awareness – would deplete him of the physical and social energies necessary to assume the spiritual and quasi-political leadership (for which he is being groomed) of the young colony. Finally, Pearl, in her function as both love and torment to her mother, perhaps most directly embodies the moral ambiguities at the heart of *The Scarlet Letter*.

As the simplifications of seeming are undercut by the intricacies of being, we look for a middle ground which might offer some accommodation to a reality as complex and ultimately indeterminate as the meaning of the symbol itself. We look for the more genuine acceptance of the social and moral conditions of life which the endings of English novels – in books as diverse as *Wuthering Heights* and *Middlemarch* – seem to make. Yet this is just where Hawthorne swerves off, elevating Hester into a representative of those Utopian hopes which obviate such accommodation to and awareness of the real world.

Pearl, humanized by her father's recognition of her, might be considered the conventional agent for such an accommodation. Like the second generation in *Wuthering Heights*, she seems finally to represent the taming of impulse which the rewards of culture necessarily demand. But Pearl is dispatched to Europe, a narrative choice which emphasizes Hawthorne's unwillingness to relinquish his hold on the American situation. For Hawthorne to have set a scene for her in the American present would have been to stress the virtues of compromise and melioration; the good-enough in the struggle between human actualities and visionary ideals. For Pearl cannot thrive as an outlaw. She needs the consistency and reciprocity which social structures foster in order to grow up. But there is no place in the world of the book where such a setting for Pearl is realized.

At the conclusion we are left not only with a sense of the dissolution of the historical Puritan commonwealth, but with no society at all as a presence to which a character might respond. The two conflicting views of experience that serve as double climax to the story would seem to provide a contrast between real and ideal social possibilities – Hester's ideal moment in the forest balanced by Arthur's more realistic one on the scaffold. Yet the society that Arthur confronts with the truth of his nature seems to disintegrate under the effect of his confession. In its place we have a multiplicity of interpretations of the enigma on his chest, and, finally, the awe surrounding the ambiguity of Hester's "A."

The final movement of the book begins with Hester walking out to the forest to meet Dimmesdale under the open sky. Here, for the first and only time, she is able to give full rein to the strength of her passion to shape life as she wishes it to be. It is her dream of human community that is dramatized here, a dream of profound intimacy between two independent, mutually responsive souls. But Dimmesdale hasn't the strength for it without her guidance. "Think for me, Hester! Thou art strong. Resolve for me!" he tells her (p. 141). Her courage and idealism overwhelm him not only because he is physically debilitated, but because he is fundamentally a creature who depends upon social institutions and order for ego support. This has often been read (and not only by feminists) as a discredit to Dimmesdale's character, but Hawthorne's point would seem to be that there are more Dimmesdales than Hesters in this world, and accommodation must be made for them in such Utopias as Hester envisages.[16] Her solution is to lead him. But however loving her motives, this merely exchanges one form of domination and control for another.

Arthur's dignity ultimately lies in his ability to recognize and dismiss what is not for him, to assert the strength of his own character by revealing it. Finding his way to the truth of his own being – the conditions of his own nature – leads him to the scaffold, where he substitutes his own version of a mutual world for Hester's. Whereas Hester's ideal connected the most intimate personal relations with the most far-flung possibilities that the "whole wide world" might hold, Arthur's spiritual vision, true to type, is expressed in the imagery of traditional Christian piety, and rooted within a publicly defined space. Its nobility lies in his effort finally to connect that emotional undertone of plaintive suffering humanity, heard in his Election Day sermon, with the rhetoric that foretells "a high and glorious destiny for the newly gathered people of the Lord" (p. 176).

For Hester, however, Arthur's version of community is as flawed as hers was for him. Thus, watching him pass her in the Election Day procession, she sees him enveloped in his worldly responsibilities and feels "there could be no real bond betwixt the clergyman and herself." And she resents him "for being able so completely to withdraw himself from their mutual world; while she groped darkly, and stretched forth her cold hands, and found him not" (p. 170.) Does Hester change her feelings on the scaffold? When Arthur asks her, "Is this not better . . . than what we dreamed of in the forest?" she responds, "I know not! . . . Better? Yea; so we may both die, and little Pearl die with us!" (p. 179). However courageous for him, Dimmesdale's action binds him to a reality that Hester may acquiesce in, but never embraces with equal fervor.

As forest and scaffold represent antithetical versions of community, we might expect them to be synthesized in Hester's return to America and her voluntary resumption of her badge. But Hester's act seems not so much a synthesis as a reformulation of the meaning of the symbol. As Arthur has shown that private acts are inevitably and inherently public ones, so Hester's dream now ramifies into a public and representative one which she shares with the sorrowing women whom she counsels. But her social work is hardly likely to serve as sublimation for her vision of what life might be. Unlike George Eliot's Dorothea, who dreams of becoming another Saint Theresa but settles for a measure of sexual and social fulfillment in her second marriage, Hester is denied any field of action commensurate with even a chastened set of ideals. Although she acknowledges that life has crippled her, she continues to hope for a future in which the ideal will absorb the actual. The emphasis is not on the flux of generations, with its potential for incremental change, but on redemption in time.

By clearing the stage, as it were, of any alternative to Hester's version of life, Hawthorne makes her the inheritor of all the novel's meanings.[17] As the structure of the town dissolves, Hester seems to have absorbed its restrictions into herself while assimilating its visionary faith to her own. With Pearl dispatched to Europe, Hester's isolation enlarges to fill all the novelistic space. Rather than thinking of her as a lonely, beleaguered soul in a society that has no use for her dreaming, we are left with an impression of the society beginning to flow toward her, seeking the wisdom of her suffering. The power relations with which the novel began are reversed. The elders have disappeared from view, while Hester, the outlaw and sinner, alone remains. Ultimately, her most significant change seems to be that she substitutes a gradualist view of redemption in time for the intensity of a personally achieved one that obliterates time, and so from an Emersonian heroine becomes a Hawthornian one.

It seems clear that Hawthorne is seeking a way to avoid the dangers of both the repressed and the revolutionary self by an exchange of energies between these two extremes within the public sphere. Assimilation is to replace isolation and so countervail the impulse toward either violent social disruption or violent self-abuse. Forest and scaffold would somehow, at some future time, merge in one grand redemptive vision. But what we have seen of human nature in this book would suggest that however conceptualized, the American dream of social perfection is defeated precisely by the "fallen" nature of the dreamers. None of the characters can meet the test of his or her aspirations. Arthur's moral cowardice mocks his spiritual ideals; Chillingworth's lust for vengeance belies his pretension to disinterested knowledge; Hester's social bravado masks an unyielding scorn for those who would necessarily be part of her new world. Each claims to be the equal of all in moral judgment and significance of being, and (until the end) each fails to make any genuine accommodation to the human needs of the other, and therefore to the human potential buried within their mutual community. Pearl's own peremptory demands for public acknowledgment of a family identity make plain the misdirection of moral energies that has occurred. Though Hester, Arthur, and Chillingworth are often read as quasi-allegorical representations of one human psyche, they can also be seen as doubles of the national dream. In this, Arthur's final act serves a critical function, designed to acknowledge and accept the necessary limitations of such ideals; yet Hester goes on assimilating it to higher aims.

Why is this emblematic ending necessary to a tale whose import seems to reject it? The sense of sacrificial suffering that the story evokes brings it close to genuine tragedy, yet we are not allowed to rest with the human condition as it is. Another identity is predicated for us – not in terms of what we are, which, putting it bluntly, Arthur has shown is hard enough to achieve, but in terms of what we might become.

The ending of *The Scarlet Letter* seems to me to represent neither a failure of judgment on Hawthorne's part nor, despite its wavering tone which borders in places on sentimental parody, an ironic condescension to Hester. For Hawthorne has invested too much in his heroine to mock her at the last. Rather, the design of the story seems to insist that tragedy and the archetype of Fall and Resurrection must somehow be made to fit each other; if the dream dies here, in the country of its last best hope, then it must be reborn in other terms. Ultimately, we are left with an unresolved tension that may go far to explain the split we find in Hawthorne's subsequent work between the tainted dark heroine, strong but burdened and limited by past sin (Zenobia, Miriam), and her pure half-sister (Priscilla, Hilda) who is indeed brushed by sorrow but not given over to it, in order that the vigil of ideal moral possibility be kept alive. Hilda sees sunshine on the mountaintops, and Hester Prynne goes on dreaming of how "sacred love should make us happy."

3
Mark Twain's Great Evasion:
Adventures of Huckleberry Finn

"He had a dream," I says, "and it shot him." "Singular dream," he says.

I

The last ten chapters of *Huckleberry Finn*, with their culmination in Huck's flight to "the Territory," have been the subject of critical controversy ever since the novel's publication.[1] The meaning of the Phelps Farm episode and its role in the novel's structure has been varyingly interpreted as a literary failure, a cheat of the reader, or a formally correct preparation for Huck's final lighting out.[2] As time has passed and *Huckleberry Finn* has settled into the status of a classic, the controversy surrounding the ending has only increased. With Huck adopted, as it were, into that family of representative character types which signify the values and ideals of our national consciousness, it becomes more imperative than ever to define his essential character and future prospects. Does Huck grow up or does he remain a boy forever? And, more pertinently, by what standards do we or should we evaluate either of these possibilities? In this regard, there is a particularly instructive comparison to be made between Huck and Pip, the English orphan hero of Charles Dickens's *Great Expectations*. In many respects their situations are alike, and will be compared in the latter portion of this chapter. But the contrasting resolution of Dickens's novel (and the differences in the pattern of experience from which it derives) helps to establish what I believe to be the distinctively American character of Mark Twain's ending.

Given the emphatically linear form of *Huckleberry Finn*, one's response to the ending depends largely upon expectations as to how Huck will act and feel derived from the preceding portions of the narrative. Yet when we, along with Huck, finally reach the Phelps Farm, our sense of what the episode is about becomes an influence operating in reverse, forcing us to reread and perhaps revise our interpretation of the preceding events in the story. Where an ambiguous ending is only a matter of a paragraph or two, a brief enigmatic scene, as in *The Scarlet Letter*, it is obviously far less subversive of the reader's sense of textual coherence than here, where the ending comprises ten chapters out of a total of forty-two, and lasts for three or four weeks of story time. Although Hester's visionary ambitions seem to me to deny the realities in which the rest of *The Scarlet Letter* is grounded, and she thereby evades a full recognition of their significance, I am not aware of any strong critical claim that the form of Hawthorne's entire novel suffers from his description of Hester's last days. In *The Scarlet Letter* the problem is rather the reverse: it lies in the discrepancy between the resolution which readers have confidently managed to impose on the book (because such a resolution "feels" right to them?) and the logic of the story which contradicts it.

Unlike the sentimental comic ending of *The House of the Seven Gables*, which has provoked much adverse criticism,[3] the ending of *The Scarlet Letter* seems to reflect the faith of many Americans that vision begins where reality fails. By denying Hester any satisfactory community within the world as we know it, Hawthorne compels the reader to live on Hester's terms. If a similar escape or evasion of reality occurs in the finale of *Huckleberry Finn*, as I believe it does, it presents itself in far more cryptic and convoluted terms, and therefore confronts the reader with a different problem of elucidation.

Let me say at the outset that I take this novel, as I do *The Scarlet Letter*, to be centrally concerned with the defeat of a visionary ideal that is at once national and individual. Quite apart from the sound of their names, the consonance between the roles of Huck Finn and Hester Prynne in the structure of their respective narratives is striking. Not only are they both outcasts, but each is abused by and alienated from paternal figures representative of social authority and order. (In Huck's case the symbolic status of these vagrants, bullies and con-men must be inferred.) While each is committed to a visionary mode of being, both are marginally but nevertheless vitally connected to the society at hand. Each maintains that connection through external forms of behavior which serve to protect and disguise a more authentic identity. Finally, neither of these social orphans ever experiences a full recognition of his or her own limitations, or moral complexities – a recognition which would inevitably defeat their exalted ideals.

However, there are significant contrasts in the fate and function of Hester and Huck which suggest changes in American society and in the quality of American optimism during the thirty years between the composition of these books. For what makes Hester ultimately the center of energy in *The Scarlet Letter* is her concentration on aspirations not yet fulfilled; she pushes toward the future and against the moral and social inheritance of a constraining past. But Huck's attention is largely focused on the imprisoning nature of shore society, rather than on his increasingly elusive goal of freedom. It is the shore scenes which dominate the book. The idyllic moments alone with Jim are only a kind of parenthesis; the weight of the narrative falls far more on criticism of what is than on delineation of what might be. Jim and Huck on the raft, though profoundly important as an antithesis, are only a sketch, as it were, for that redemptive American community which the shore has betrayed.

Moreover, in *The Scarlet Letter* Hester's person is not only of continuing concern to the Boston elders, but she occupies a designated social space which the entire town acknowledges. Ultimately, her suffering gives her a mysterious, even sacred aura. And her vision has the power to move others. Not only can she articulate it to herself, but, at the last, she shares it with the women who seek comfort from her in their troubles. For at least some members of her dissolving community she has a voice. But Huck has no recognizable meaning or value for his group.[4] Although he can spin out fictions to save his life, he has a deadly fear of speaking the truth. It is therefore a fitting pathos that he can only rejoin society at the Phelps Farm by dying to himself, to be reborn as that Sunday-school bad boy Tom Sawyer. He ends with Tom the only auditor of his adventures – Tom whom he knows to be full of lies. The loving intimacy of his experience with Jim will never be revealed to any community within the book. There is no scaffold in the marketplace, no center of public life where one might confess and hope to be heard. As the Phelps episode makes clear, such a social possibility had become unthinkable to Mark Twain. And yet to leave Huck's future to the obsessive machinations of Tom Sawyer is to give up hope entirely. So we are faced with what might be called an over-determined double ending. With reality on the Phelps Farm given an excruciatingly bitter comic burial, Huck, dead to himself, is reborn once more in an escape from all social bonds and from any permanent human connection. Keeping one step ahead of the rest, he lights out for the territory – a gesture which, most tellingly, has become a cultural shibboleth for the integrity of individual vision.

Huck has been defined as a true radical and revolutionary of a non-traditional antinomian type, without any notion of allegiance to a higher law. As Robert Penn Warren puts it, Huck's "ethic is based on a long humble scrutiny of experience," his integrity reasserted "in the absolute antinomianism of *flight*." On the face of it, this might seem an accurate description of Huck's final condition, but Warren himself questions the flight as a satisfactory resolution of the confrontation between ideal and real which underlies events at the Phelps Farm asking, "Should the novel be taken to deny the necessity of community?"[5] The proposition that I hope to demonstrate is just the converse. It is the failure of shore society (given its quietus in the satire at the farm) that deepens the desire for ideal community and so makes the flight of the last line *appear* as a regenerative act, despite the fact that Huck's "absolute antinomianism" is hardly promising ground upon which to construct either a social or individual ideal.[6]

In my reading, the Phelps Farm episode is quite the opposite of that 'happy ending' which has been the subject of some well-known critical objections. To consider it either as happy, or meaningless (another variant), is to disregard the multiple contradictions it contains between tone and event; the ironies which mock a false morality as well as a false taste in fiction and which anticipate Brecht in the bitterness of their implication that happy endings belong only to the realm of literary romance.[7]

In fact, by the time we arrive at the Phelps Farm, the terms "ideal" and "real," apparently symbolized in the opposing geography of river and shore, have actually become so entwined with one another that they seem to have exchanged places. If real refers to the world of sense and natural feeling, to a life that can be tested on the pulses, so to speak, then the naked simplicity of Huck's life with Jim on the raft, although keyed to the harmonies of an idyll, is actually the most palpably real experience in the book. There is more felt life in the dialogue between the runaway boy and the escaped slave, and in Huck's lyrical recollections of their shared experience, than anywhere else in the novel. On the other hand, if the ideal refers to a dreamlike mental construct, an idea of perfection, then its debased form lies in the sentimentalized, factitious life of the shore inhabitants, where hospitality precedes ritual slaughter, and the distinction between a dead pet and a murdered child is dissolved in the cult of tears. The interchangeable masks of false identity that Huck dons on shore (regularly forgetting what his name is supposed to be) perfectly reflect the abstract, conventionalized behavior of the people he encounters. His distanced observer's stance underscores the dreamlike irrationality of their life. It is precisely this latter image of quotidian social life as a debased, third-rate fiction which culminates in the burlesque of the ending, with Tom Sawyer the presiding genius of inanity.

If Karl Marx's dictum that all great events and characters of world history occur twice, first as tragedy, then as farce, can be imagined as having an analogue within a fictional history, the farcical ending of this narrative might be seen as a case in point. For nowhere in the book is Twain's extensive use of parallel passages that contrast in tone more marked than in the relation between its beginning and ending. Through a kind of black parody, the major themes of the story (evasion, disguise, imprisonment, escape and rebirth) as well as many minor motifs, established in the first section of the book (up to the escape from Jackson's Island) are recapitulated here in a ludicrous *dénouement* which does nothing so much as reinforce one's sense of those barbarous conditions of social existence to which Huck has borne witness all along.

As the modest vernacular style of the preceding portions of the book supports the weight of a tragic truth – the implicit failure of the journey – so the ending presents us with its bitterly comic inversion. It is as if Mark Twain were saying: Only in a society of willing victims and fools could such a bogus ending be believed. And further, that America's view of itself, of its special destiny among nations, is itself only another con-game out of historical romance. If you are foolish enough to live by such fictions, then you will believe that Miss Watson's deathbed conversion creates a happy ending, and be equally successful in conning yourself into ignoring every cruel absurdity that Tom invents to orchestrate it. Mark Twain's burlesque of literary romance and boy's adventure is only the screen for a deeper attack on an American society that has failed to realize its own promise of moral and social rebirth.[8]

In his biography of Clemens, Justin Kaplan cites the often-repeated incident of the abortive Whittier birthday speech in which Mark Twain, in the guise of a joke, managed to call the elders of the genteel literary establishment – Emerson, Holmes and Longfellow – frauds. Kaplan points out that by this time (December, 1877), Mark Twain had moved away from "benign entertainment and toward highly complex and conflictive comic molds." Although his satire expressed his growing sense of independence and alienation from established values, the hostility of its "content, as it seems now, was too painful for him to acknowledge consciously." To free himself of the charge of intentional insult he relied on the mixture of innocence and self-mockery which he had early developed in his public lecture persona. Innocence allowed him to deny conscious responsibility, self-mockery enabled him to turn his own humiliations into a weapon against his audience's pretensions and self-delusions.[9] It would seem that as the satiric component of Mark Twain's humor deepened, his dependence on strategies of disguise grew stronger. However, in the construction of the ending of *Huckleberry Finn*, that delicate balance between innocence, self-mockery, and social satire, which has served the narrative very well thus far, seems to have gone awry. For in the obsessive moral humiliation which he visits upon Huck and Jim, jettisoning their characters as we have come to know them, Mark Twain appears to have become trapped in the coils of his own disguise. Whether in an excess of rage or anxiety, his attack on his audience seems bought at the cost of his own humanity.[10]

A further way of approaching the phenomenon of disguise, which played such an important role both in Twain's life and work, is to consider it more directly in terms of the mechanism which Freud defined as "the joke-work." As Freud gave the name "dream-work" to the totality of "transforming processes" which make manifest the dream images of latent dream thoughts, so he used the term "joke-work" to describe similar processes – abbreviation, compression, substitute formation – which he found in the action of jokes.[11]

So the comic biographies which Huck invents throughout the river journey to protect his secret life with Jim also enable him to stand by, while a surrogate figure (Buck Grangerford, Boggs's daughter) enacts the fate which might be imagined to be his, should he remain on shore. This dramatic displacement of feeling merges with another even more pervasive – and therefore less noticeable – form of disguise, which is the stylistic mark of Huck's narrative voice. This, of course, is the tradition of the backwoods, deadpan humorist, the innocent and bewildered bystander, which Mark Twain brought to sophisticated perfection in his platform monologues, and which bears a relation to the content of social satire similar to that which the dreamer has to the images of his own dreams.[12] In both instances the observer is dissociated (and therefore protected) from the real import as well as the affect of the events which he is observing. As a psychological strategy, it not only serves to protect one from pain (as Kaplan notes), but also from any imperative to act or struggle for change which conscious awareness might entail. Moreover Huck's narrative innocence on the river only flatters the reader's sense of his own superior acumen. It offers ready assurance that one has hold of the full significance of each episode. For it is clear that we are being invited to seek a meaning and an emotion in Huck's words other than his own deadpan accounting. The silences that direct us toward what ought to be rather than what is are clearly marked.

Through this aspect of the style, then, the reader's vantage point is subtly reinforced. Morally speaking, our better nature is engaged by sympathy with Huck's revelations and the revulsion from shore life which they arouse. But our own complicity in these social failings, the dubious in our own inner lives, is not directly challenged. It is all too easy to read the first two-thirds of *Huckleberry Finn* while maintaining, along with Huck, an us-and-them attitude toward the world it depicts.

However, this pattern does not hold true for the ending. In the final episode, as Huck assumes Tom Sawyer's name, his own comic mask drops away. There is no longer any distance between him and his world. Here, not a character alone but the burlesque itself becomes a kind of totalizing joke-work whose displacements and substitutions mock reader and characters alike. With the tension between Huck and his world dissolved, the major characters disappear into the plot, and the author (already masked as that literary personage Mark Twain), through the sudden importation of Tom Sawyer, seems himself to take over the action. In all, Mark Twain's overmastering intention seems to be the subversion of any common ground between socially determined conventions of thought, speech, literary form (including the one he has made use of throughout the book) and human emotional needs.

The authentic feeling which has arisen between Huck and Jim, based upon mutual respect for one another's integrity, dies on the Phelps Farm. As opposed to all the weak, corrupt, and fairly insane fathers we have seen on shore, Jim has been the ideal – nurturer, friend, protector, and moral tutor in one. But once at the farm their personal bond is obliterated from Huck's consciousness as he, Jim, and Tom conform their relations to the pattern of their days at Miss Watson's. However, although the Phelps Farm is akin to life at Miss Watson's, these chapters afford no simple drama of return. For Jim, allowed some comforts at the beginning of his imprisonment here, is eventually reduced to a condition of misery and exploitation far worse than anything he endured at the outset of the story. If at Miss Watson's he was a clever but superstitious slave, here he assumes the role, for Huck and Tom as well as for us, of an abused gull. His childlike awe of Tom and continued trust in Huck only deepen the humiliation to which Twain subjects him.

What is striking about the main parallel actions of the beginning and ending – kidnapping and imprisonment of Huck by a con-man (his father), kidnapping and imprisonment of Jim by the duke and king – is that the course of the journey has so altered our conception of the reciprocal humanity of Jim and Huck that we are repelled here, as we would not necessarily have been in the first chapter, by seeing Jim used as a prop in a boys' game. In other words, Jim here occupies the same position and is in potentially the same danger as Huck was *vis à vis* his father. One was depicted in realistic vernacular terms. The other, utilizing Jim's shore persona of ignorant 'darky,' is played for a joke. But now the joke only heightens the inhumanity of treating a human being as if he were a counter in a game. Moreover, the journey has educated us to see that this inhumanity toward Jim is only a more extreme version of the exploitative relations that pervade every other shore episode – the Shepherdson-Grangerford feud, where killing enhances male vanity and pride; the Arkansas lynch mob, where Boggs's death serves the crowd's appetite for drama; the Wilks's funeral 'orgies,' where Anglophile snobbery enables the con-men to prey on the pretensions and greed of an entire town. All of these incidents are funny as well as horrific, and each evokes a measure of sympathy for the folly of the protagonists. The distinction of the ending is that its antics are neither funny nor engaging but merely grotesque. That, I believe, is its point. At the end of the journey the fictional comforts of verisimilitude entirely break down, and with them any possibility of an emotionally consistent world. Instead, 'reality' is perceived to be nothing but a violent and dangerous masquerade. Tom's 'fun' ends in a nightmare posse of local farmers eager to kill him in order to protect the Phelps's investment in Jim's return to his putative master.

Much has been written about Jim's slavery, especially in relation to the ending.[13] And, indeed, the increasing harshness of Jim's treatment, as well as his own regression, suggests an historical parallel to the worsening conditions for blacks as the nineteenth century wore on. However, the larger issue of the book is the mental and moral enslavement which is the lot of everyone in this society: so while Jim's condition underlines the hypocritical inhumanity of a particular era, it cannot be separated, except by degree, from those more comprehensive cultural failings that the Thirteenth Amendment did not abolish. Jim is the necessary extreme – at once the most complete social and legal victim and yet the freest to live naturally within himself. Cast out by the society that exploits him, he is left alone to define his own moral life, and in so doing to serve as a measure for Huck's. If his slavery becomes one term in a series of related images of enslavement, this is not to deny the dramatic impact of his condition. Nothing is so damning to the visionary ideal which America proposes for itself as its actual treatment of racial minorities, beginning with blacks and Indians. But this is also why Jim's aborted escape into free territory (which has been of concern to many readers) is a false issue in terms of the subject matter of the book – as if Mark Twain in 1876 had set out to recapitulate *Uncle Tom's Cabin*. Rather, Jim's enslavement and subsequent humiliation bespeak Twain's overwhelming revulsion (behind the comic mask) from all manifestations of shore life. Jim provides an image of the infernal conditions which lie in wait for Huck should he actually give up his identity and become Tom Sawyer.

For in assimilating himself with Tom, Huck becomes the traducer of that self which had flourished on the river under the tutelage of Jim. In effect, he becomes one of the ghosts he has always feared, one of those intimations of another self which threatens the integrity of the nascent ego. So he stands by while Jim, trusting in his presence, submits himself to Tom's ambitious cruelties, while Tom crows triumphantly that "it was the best fun he ever had in his life . . . and if he only could see his way to it we would keep it up all the rest of our lives and leave Jim to our children to get out; for he believed Jim would come to like it better and better the more he got used to it."[14] The Huck who responds to Aunt Sally's query about the fictitious steamboat accident – "Good gracious! Anybody hurt?" "No'm. Killed a nigger." "Well, it's lucky; because sometimes people do get hurt." (p. 185) – is a figure who has so instinctively resumed the false skin of his shore 'conscience' at the appearance of his shore 'home' that even before he finds out who he is ("It was like being born again, I was so glad to find out who I was") there is little prospect that here he could ever be anyone but Tom Sawyer.

On shore Huck has always disbelieved his own powers, but here his awe and admiration of Tom make him nearly as impotent as Jim. In fact, once they accept Tom's direction, Huck and Jim become as dependent upon him for the resolution of their common fate as Tom himself is on "the best authorities." In each case, the subject's piety enhances the satire. Just as Tom is the fool of his literary 'principles,' so Huck and Jim become his fools. The nadir of this benighted subservience is surely the sight we are given of Jim temporarily freed in order to collect another prop for his imprisonment. With Tom supervising, Jim and Huck roll a heavy grindstone back to the cabin for Jim to chisel on it the mournful inscriptions that stimulate Tom's tears.

Because Mark Twain prevents Huck from acknowledging the cruelty of Tom Sawyer's games, Huck is denied the option of consciously rejecting Tom as a social model and, therefore, of entertaining any alternative shore identity for himself. With his social self given over to Tom's dominion, and Tom standing as metaphor for the cast of mind of an entire society, Huck has no choice, if he is to break free of the Tom in himself, but to reject 'civilization' in toto. The bitterness here derives from Mark Twain's insistence that there is no exit from this hellish maze because cultural forms not only distort moral intentions but the shape of consciousness itself – the sense we carry in us of who and what we are.[15]

Having engineered this syllogism, Mark Twain plays the role which Hank Morgan will later assume against the chivalry of sixth-century England.[16] Like "The Battle of the Sand-Belt," 'The Evasion' is a kind of authorial blow-up. Like Hank Morgan, Mark Twain uses his own technological tools – language and literary form – to destroy the world that resists his dream, and like the holocaust that ends by consuming the Connecticut Yankee, here too the destruction of possibility has a near-apocalyptical completeness to it.[17]

The sense of the entire episode as a kind of blasphemy, at least a blasting, of the mutual world Jim and Huck have created is intensified by the juxtaposition, just before this, of Huck's memory of Jim on the river – perhaps the most compelling image in the book. It is a visual recollection in which Huck's characteristically quiet idiom expands to capture something of the rhythm and tone of the Jubilee singing which Mark Twain is said to have enjoyed:[18]

... and I see Jim before me, all the time, in the day, and in the night-time, sometimes moonlight, sometimes storms, and we a-floating along, talking, and singing, and laughing ...   (p. 179)

The passage continues with Huck's recollection of scenes, encapsulating the flow of their entire river journey and galvanizing him into his climactic decision to go to Hell and rescue Jim. The irony is that once on shore, at the gates of Hell, Huck must become a ghost of himself – divest himself of his 'natural' parts. What these metaphoric terms mean is that there is no correlative shore life which can give his river imagery social texture or meaning. There is no possibility of Huck taking his wisdom back into society.

In retrospect, we can see that self-division was always the functional principle of Huck's character. He can't stand being "sivilized," but loneliness drives him back to Tom Sawyer and his robber games. As Richard Poirier points out, "Tom Sawyer's games are intimately related . . . to the respectable aspects of adult society." The necessary condition for membership in Tom's gang is that Huck return to the Widow Douglas. The metaphoric suggestion is that " 'respectable' society as represented by the Widow is equivalent to a 'band of robbers'."[19]

It is his connection to Jim that enables Huck to express the antithetical side of his own nature. Alone, it is doubtful whether he would have gone so far as to leave Jackson's Island on a raft. It would have been more characteristic of him to remain a few yards off-shore, hiding in the woods, watching the river boats go by, and sneaking back at night for contact with Tom. For Huck's choices, even once on the river, are never final ones. The anxiety associated with his socialized shore "conscience," as well as his instinctive submission to the power of circumstance to determine the outcome of events, perhaps explains the quality of reprise in the decision of Chapter 31 to commit himself to Jim's rescue, when we might have thought this issue had been settled for him once before.

Unlike Jim, who is an absolute outsider and whose peril is the catalyst for Huck's going into action, the boy has the power to utilize verbal disguise, to dress himself in the fictions which complement his conventional appearance. His pathos is that although able to travel between two worlds, he is unable to achieve any internal mediation between the commitments and values which divide them. As he embodies the two opposing principles of received morality and natural law which dominate the book's structure, so Huck is representative of the problem of America itself – forever caught between the forms that history has actually taken there, and the desire for what might have been, for that freedom of social possibility which, for a moment, Jim and Huck together seem to create in the wilderness of the raft.

The dichotomy between these two realms of experience is intensified by the manner in which Huck and Jim suppress their relationship once the duke and king invade their territory. If "the raft is like America itself," as Poirier acutely suggests,[20] then with the arrival of the refugee con artists the nation's moral potential is complete. As Michael J. Hoffman points out, the duke and king operate by turning society's standard social responses against itself: by using conventional emotions and tastes to fleece and swindle. Role players *par excellence*, they mirror the pretensions and delusions of those on whom they prey.[21] Once they take charge, subverting the welcome offered them, the original ideal of a just and loving community based on the dignity of each goes underground. So Jim masquerades as Huck's "nigger," and both become servants and outcasts again – sleeping outside their own tent in the rain. Huck, who recognizes from the first that the duke and king are Pap's "kind of people," acccommodates to them in order to keep family peace: "What you want above all things on a raft, is for everybody to be satisfied, and feel right and kind towards the others" (p. 106). As all four are runaways and outcasts, they are plausible constituents of a New World community that inevitably contains both worst and best. But as Mark Twain dramatizes it, there is no possible middle ground, no dialectic that can bridge the moral extremes which these opposed pairs represent. Rather, they exist in the same kind of nightmare tandem (the duke and king keep turning up just when Huck and Jim think they are "shut of them") as do Huck's spontaneous moral feelings with the imperatives of his socialized conscience.

With the con-men bringing onto the raft all the ills from which Huck and Jim sought escape, the raft begins to look like a structural counterpart of Hawthorne's Boston. As they drift south toward the Phelps Farm, and farther than ever from the "freedom" which was their initial goal, the possibility of Huck and Jim salvaging any fragment of their idyll together becomes even more remote than the fleeting hopes which gleamed for Hester and Arthur in the forest.

If the duke and king destroy the pleasures of the raft, social existence as it is conceived on shore is even more frightening and dangerous for Huck. The shore is a kind of charnel house in which all fathers are either impotent bullies who invite attack, like Pap and Boggs, or vain, cold-blooded killers, like Grangerford and Sherburn. It is telling that when Huck leaves the raft, not only must Jim hide in order to protect himself, but Huck's awareness of him also disappears. It is as if Jim's "laying low" were the metaphoric equivalent of Huck's psychic repression of him; as if the horrors of the shore demanded the most absolute inner defenses. Because on shore Huck has no recall of river life, there is no possibility that he can integrate the two aspects of himself. Instead, we get a comic displacement of his feelings which express longings he cannot otherwise confront.

In the circus scene following Boggs's death, an ugly reality is transformed into the charm of a wish-fulfillment dream. Having seen the drunk Boggs stumble into town, disruptive and bullying but essentially harmless, and then seen him coldly wiped out by Colonel Sherburn while the townspeople stand aside, clustered together like dumb sheep, Huck has seen enough. He goes to the circus where all is graceful and harmoniously arranged, audience and performers sympathetically attuned. Into their midst a drunk man appears, stirring up the audience with his demand to ride a horse. People in the crowd begin to threaten him while the ringmaster pleads for order. The man gets on the horse and appears to be in grave danger, first hanging from one side, then the other. However, as he proceeds he reveals a marvellous skill. Shedding seventeen suits of clothes while standing upright on the galloping horse, he reveals himself to be slim and handsome. The audience howl with pleasure; Huck is dumbfounded, thinking the ringmaster was tricked. But we see that all this is simply part of a pre-ordained plot in which each of the principals has an assigned role. Huck's guilelessness would seem to mask a deeper wish for those happy fictions that would transform the miseries of Pap and Boggs into the frank and artful illusion of a successful performance. But this uncommon moment is buried in a welter of those cruel and tyrannical self-delusions which most typify shore life.

That Huck will never achieve the inner balance and social trust symbolized by the relation between the bare-back rider and his audience is made clear in his farewell to Mary Jane Wilks. Occurring just before his arrival at the Phelps Farm, it must be considered his conclusive rejection of any resting-place on shore. As at several other points in the story, a window, dark or lighted, symbolizes Huck's conflict between home-longings and fears of entrapment:

No light there; the house all dark – which made me feel sorry and disappointed; I don't know why. But at last, just as I was sailing by, *flash* comes the light in Mary Jane's window! and my heart swelled up like to burst; and the same second the house and all was behind me in the dark, and wasn't ever going to be before me no more in this world. (p. 171)

The Wilks episode is the only one of the three major shore encounters in which there is a personal temptation for Huck to remain. As the last of the series, his escape here leaves him most emphatically in a realm of darkness and loneliness, the motif with which the Phelps Farm sequence begins.

There is nothing in its opening (Chapter 32) to suggest the burlesque that follows. The tone of quiet observation, the evocations of loneliness and death are all in Huck's familiar idiom, one that particularly recalls the opening scene at the Widow's, when he sat alone by the window in his room looking out at the stars and waiting for Tom Sawyer to rescue him. That Huck's arrival has the force of a conclusion is conveyed both by the slower opening pace of this episode, as compared with the others en route, and the observations themselves with the suggestive echo of an all too familiar past.[22]

Unlike Huck's previous shore forays, here he does not find himself in the midst of a new situation before he half understands it. This time he has scouted out the neighborhood; he knows where he is and what he wants to do. But the pause in the narrative, which allows him to take in the atmosphere of the farm, casts an ominous shadow over his intentions. The day has a hot, bright, Sunday-like stillness. Bugs drone, leaves rustle; there is, however, no sense of well-being. Huck thinks of mourning and wishes he were dead and done for. The empty farmstead, with all hands gone to the fields, looks like hundreds of others he has known. Nothing about its fenced plot or its snug log houses pleases his eye or evokes feelings of comfort. Instead, these images of a provincial utilitarian world, culminating in the ancient wail of a spinning wheel somewhere far indoors, fill him with a sense of oppression and despair. The boredom, the monotony of this life of constricted spaces is overwhelming.

In these opening paragraphs, the shore world, which had at least afforded Huck the stimulus of new adventures, now resolves once again into its most recognizable and predictable shape. As the plot is about to reveal, the downstream trip has carried Huck back to a simulacrum of the place from which he originally sought escape. But the traditional pattern of return, with its reward of self-renewal and/or public recognition, is short-circuited. Even when Tom Sawyer puts everything to rights at the last, there is no sense that the Huck of the raft and the Huck of the shore are even on speaking terms. It is therefore fitting that Huck's return should be initiated by a false rebirth – not into a deeper part of himself, as occurred when he escaped his unnatural father and found a natural one in Jim, but into the persona who was the inspiration for all his fictional identities on shore.

To get a closer look at the structure of meaning which leads to the debacle at the Phelps Farm, I want to return to the subject of jokes and examine some other aspects of their role in the actions and events of the narrative. Here I am, somewhat artificially and incompletely, distinguishing between those consciously-enacted tricks and games associated with Huck, Tom, and the con-men, and the broader, metaphorical usage which shades off from these into the self-tricking, self-deluding practices of shore society at large.

If we compare the significance of jokes in the three main sections of the book – the escape from Jackson's Island, the entire river journey with itc salternating rhythm of shore and raft, the Phelps Farm conclusion – we can understand better the function of the ending as a barrier to any form of self and social reintegration; that is, as a denial of the possibility of achieving a middle ground for Huck.

In Chapter 2 Tom and Huck sneak up on Miss Watson's "big nigger, named Jim" who is sitting under a tree near the kitchen doorway, snoozing. Tom wants to tie him to the tree and "play something on him." They settle for slipping off his hat and hanging it from an overhead limb. When Jim wakes, he is convinced that he has been overtaken by spirits. He elaborates the event into a heroic tale of "having seen the devil and been rode by witches." Although the joke is childishly insensitive, Jim is imaginative enough to profit from it ("Niggers would come miles to hear Jim tell about it" [p. 7]), and a rough *quid pro quo* is maintained. The reader's concern, which may be aroused by Jim's gullibility and ignorance, is thereby relaxed. Jim can take care of himself. He is savvy enough to find his own profit in the story. The apparent equivalence between the powerless boys and the slave allows them to engage in a kind of mock social bargain which apes those made by the adult world. The exchange-value of jokes, as it were, thus serves as an index to the quality of response, as of responsibility, which binds individuals in this society to one another. For the powerless on shore, jokes provide a substitute form of social profit – just as later, in the hands of the con-men jokes become a tool for more direct material profit – and profit is the determining principle of shore relationships. Thus Huck's value to his father is not too far removed from Jim's value to Miss Watson. She claims to worry about Jim's soul and conducts evening prayers for her slaves, but she can't resist the opportunity to sell Jim for eight hundred dollars when an offer comes along. So Pap Finn, in a parody of genteel morals, lathers himself about Huck's upbringing in order to get his hands on the boy's cash. Whether from conscious cruelty or social conditioning, no one in this society is free of exploitative motives.

Furthermore, if to live on shore is to become enmeshed in a

variety of pious and hypocritical fictions, to be one's own con-man, so to speak, then the only semblance of freedom available is to confront one set of fictions with another. This is the virtue for Huck of Tom's games. But on Jackson's Island, where genuine intimacy and mutual concern spring up between Huck and Jim, jokes have a different significance.

Huddled with Jim inside their cave, Huck, having been exposed to real danger (facing his father behind the barrel of a shot-gun) and catapulted into real escape (contriving his own murder), finds himself initiated into an authentic adventure far removed from those pirate fantasies of Tom's which they once enacted together on the island. The mode of existence which Huck and Jim undertake is both natural and (in the context of their shore life) extraordinary. Each is immediately comfortable with the other and immediately recognizes the other as a fellow outcast. Theirs is a human, not an economic, bargain as they salve each other's loneliness and fear. Jim assumes his role of protector and nurturer. While he lies low, Huck becomes explorer and go-between, the mediating link with the shore. Before they leave the island, the structure of their future relationship is established.

It is only after days of lazing together that Huck injects a typical joke from Tom Sawyer's world into theirs. He puts a dead rattlesnake on Jim's bed, "thinking there'd be some fun when Jim found him there" (p. 45). Unfortunately, the live mate turns up, bites Jim badly, and Jim suffers four painful, feverish days. Once assimilated to the natural world of both human emotions and physical landscape, jokes like all other events have unforeseen consequences; the pain they cause is real. It is only on shore, where people behave as if they were mindless creations of some derivative fiction, that actions may exist in a weightless limbo where human beings, when pricked, hardly seem to bleed. It is precisely through Huck's intrusion of the jokes of one world into another that he learns to discriminate between the moral implications of each.

But he does learn this, as we also do, in the climactic "trashing" scene (Chapter 15) where he is all too ready to debunk Jim's love and concern for his safety ("En ycu ain' dead — You ain' drowned. . . . Lemme look at you, Chile, lemme feel o' you" [p. 71]) by a trick which would turn Jim into the fool of his own superstitious nature. But it is Jim who turns the tables and gives the moral lesson here. The passage, with its celebrated rebuke of

Huck, provides us with an ineradicable image of Jim's human dignity:

"En when I wake up en fine you back agin' . . . de tears come en I could a got down on my knees en kiss' you' foot I's so thankful. En all you wuz thinkin' bout wuz how you could make a fool uv old Jim wid a lie. Dat truck dah is *trash*; en trash is what people is dat puts dirt on de head er dey fren's en makes 'em ashamed."

. . . It was fifteen minutes before I could work myself up to go and humble myself to a nigger – but I done it, and I warn't ever sorry for it afterwards, neither.   (p. 74)

After Huck humbles himself to Jim there is no more thought of exploiting the slave's credulity. Jim's predilection for magic, which was an acceptable object of fun at Miss Watson's, is now so entwined with the dignity of his personal feeling that it is Huck, not Jim, who is in danger of seeming the real fool.

The alienation between the two worlds of the book – encapsulated in its dual comic and lyric styles – deepens with the arrival of the con-men. For when the duke and king turn up, jokes, which at least had begun in a kind of careless innocence to while away the boredom of shore life, take on a sordid, even sinister cast. In mirroring the life of the shore, the pretenders point up the moral imbecility at its heart. After the Wilks episode, they blame each other, drinking and snarling, for their misfortunes – even as thieves they are shoddy failures. Lacking the courage to fight, they fall instead on their whiskey bottles and nurse themselves into a stupor in each other's arms, like a pair of grotesque infants in a parody of brotherly love.

Given these antitheses, it is striking that the ending should return us to a world entirely under the dominion of Tom Sawyer's remorseless appetite for jokes. Here, there is no contest, no tension between two opposing images of experience, much less an effort to fuse them into one comprehensive perspective. Tom's games are no longer fancies bred on the margin of the adult world of St Petersburg and so constrained, at least, by the traditional authority of judges, school teachers, and ministers. The overtones of social anarchy, beginning with Huck's murderous conflict with his father and running through all the succeeding shore episodes – where revenge, lynching, and trial by acclamation displace legitimate forms of civil authority – culminate on the Phelps Farm in the Saturnalia of Tom's rule.[23]

The most curious part of Tom's enslavement to his illusions is that no one offers him any opposition. Unlike his great prototype, Don Quixote, Tom suffers no ridicule or abuse for the sake of his dreams. Instead, it is his victims who suffer. Just as Colonel Sherburn mocks the lynch mob as a bunch of fools and cowards, so Tom turns the entire farm population and their neighbors into his fools. (Since he too is "enslaved" by forms that express an inhumane disregard for another's suffering, his power, like that of all the shore bullies, becomes the measure of his own morally crippled state.)

Nor, once the truth of Tom's "Evasion" is revealed, is there anyone to criticize him for prolonging Jim's captivity, for risking Jim's life with his plotting, or for humiliating Jim with his games. Even Tom's outraged pronouncement that Jim has been free all along is not made out of compassion or gratitude to Jim for sacrificing his chance of escape in order to nurse Tom's wound, but because the rules of Tom's game prescribe a particular outcome – Jim should be freed.

What would Tom have done if he, Huck, and Jim had got away on the raft? They would have had "adventures plumb to the mouth of the river." Then Tom would have told Jim he'd been free all along and paid him for his time. So the Evasion would finally coincide with the truth (which is, perhaps, the faith that makes for happy endings). As it is, Jim is paid off – forty dollars, exactly the price the duke and king got for betraying him, and exactly the price that Huck received from the slave hunters to whom he almost betrayed Jim (Chapter 16). Circulating within the text, the sum takes on the force of a symbol. Its ironic allusion to the biblical exodus from slavery, which lasted forty years in the wilderness but resulted in the sight of the Promised Land, comments on the material greed that underlies America's betrayal of its dream of itself as another redeemer nation. We hear that Jim is happy with his money. We remember the pathos of his assertion on Jackson's Island that he is rich because he finally owns himself. If he has feelings about the distinction between taking and being given freedom, we will never know. By this time the book's moral tension has run out.

Perhaps now we can see better the strategy that precipitates the reversal of the last line. Without Huck's resurrection the book would fall into what Robert M. Adams has called, in a different context, "a complete and vindictive nihilism" – a kind of narrative suicide in which life is shown to be in conflict with its own assumptions.[24] And, paradoxically, it is this complete annihilation of society that prepares us, not only to empathize with Huck's flight, but to accept it as having cultural as well as individual meaning. For at the very end, society as a structure of relations, a web of voices and values, has once more disappeared. There is no voice left in the book but Huck's, no point of view to cling to but his. The distinctively American aspect of Huck's antinomianism resonates in the phrase that forecasts his future: part leader, part prey, his ambiguous relation to others lies in his strategy of keeping "one step ahead of of the rest."

But before we allow ourselves to slide into the facile conclusion that Huck's flight is a triumph for representative heroism, or, indeed, for individualism in any form, we must give more precise attention to the significance of his relation to Tom and Tom's function in his imaginative life. Throughout the journey Tom has served as Huck's social alter-ego, an image of competence and survival to which Huck turns whenever anxiety, aroused by loneliness and home-longings, threatens to entrap him. Tom's image then reveals the depth of Huck's attraction to shore life. For though Tom seeks to evade adult society, he wishes, in fact, to rule over it and so belong to it in the most intimate way possible. Indeed, his fantasies on the Phelps Plantation can be read as a metaphoric expression of the fate of the Emersonian theme when it became a justification for material self-aggrandizement and monopoly capitalism, as it had in Twain's own day. Tom, here, is only a step away from the patron saint of Jay Gatsby's youth, the robber baron Jim Hill – whose epithet also suggests the American penchant for masking the facts of industrialism in the trappings of romance.

Huck's longing for Tom then is as much an acknowledgment of an alternative, or fantasied, part of himself, as it is a desire to evade the claims of his own moral nature by merging his identity with Tom's. Yet, if Tom represents the only imaginable freedom available within society, the freedom to dominate others, it is no wonder that Huck is frightened of what it means to be "sivilized." For when he has seen such behavior enacted in realistic terms – in the Feud and the killing of Boggs – it has made him sick. Moreover, the contrast between Tom's and Huck's fantasies emphasizes the radical moral distinction which divides the boys.

Huck's fictions are spontaneous creations, determined by the events of the moment, while Tom's plots are never his own inventions. Their elaborate prescriptions indulge his narcissism, because within them he can inflate to monstrous and absurd proportions, losing all touch with the limitations of his own being. As his fictions have no pragmatic function, one generates another purely for the pleasure it brings imaginatively to dominate others. In this sense Tom is a proto-artist, which makes his reduction of human beings to mere artifacts all the more chilling. Huck, on the other hand, though he too takes pleasure in developing plots, never uses his stories to dominate a group, only to protect himself and Jim from attack. His characteristic mode of accommodation is to make himself smaller, to give up some of his own autonomy (as he does his tent to the con-men) in order to avoid the consequences of social confrontation. The fact that Tom's fantasies are played out in safe circumstances – Jim has already been freed, Aunt Sally is a foolish and forgiving soul – suggests the depth of Tom's allegiance to and trust in the protection of the shore world – something Huck, with his chronic fear of the predatory nature of others, never feels. About Tom's bogus plot to free the slave he knew was already free, Huck says: "and I couldn't ever understand before, until . . . that talk, how he could help set a nigger free, with his bringing-up" (p. 243). Surely, one of the functions of the Phelps Farm episode is to disabuse Huck of the hope that he could ever merge with Tom Sawyer and still remain himself. If Tom is Huck's alter-ego, then Huck's flight is all the more certainly a recoil from those socially focused desires that he can neither accept nor overcome.

However, those who would see in Huck's final "lighting out" a redemption or resurrection of the earlier, morally engaged Huck of the river sequences, are forced to diminish the meaning of the Phelps Farm experience in the structure of the book. For the Phelps episode makes clear the impossibility for Huck of ever achieving a visionary ideal based on those energies nurtured on the raft – energies which direct our attention toward a goal that might be socially as well as individually regenerative. In the brief meetings which occur here between Huck and Jim, it is only in Jim's response that we glimpse the memory of the former bond between them. Like a good American, Huck shucks off his past; forgetting, a prime form of evasion, is one of the marks of his nature.

T. S. Eliot, identifying Huck with the natural force of the river, said, "Huck Finn must come from nowhere and be bound for nowhere. . . . He has no beginning and no end."[25] This defines Huck in terms akin to those of the Whitmanesque cosmic myth, and, indeed, Eliot likened him to Whitman's persona of the loafer. But again, to posit such a view of Huck is to ignore the self-division which he, unlike Whitman, makes no effort to overcome. Huck's integrity may finally lie in the truth of what he leaves unresolved, not in what he claims to transcend.

Nevertheless, to deny half of oneself, as Huck is forced to do at the end, is not to strengthen but to impoverish creative possibilities. What is left to a person whose energies are forever concentrated in flight? As Hawthorne makes clear, a self without any significant relationships is hardly a self at all. Huck's final flight, then, does not so much reverse the meanings of the Phelps Farm as offer an alternative to them, one that is a profoundly equivocal recoil from the impossibility of things as they are. Where can one go to evade an untrustworthy and duplicitous world that threatens one's integrity? Huck takes the characteristic American route and turns toward a metaphoric wilderness – that vaguely delineated "territory" which is, indeed, nowhere.

Huck and Tom are antithetical parts of one another, polar opposites rather than twins. Neither grows up because neither confronts the other portion of his being. The reader who shares this view will not be surprised to learn that in subsequent notes for stories resurrecting Huck, Mark Twain always had him paired with Tom. For example, two old men return from their wanderings, mourn the past "and agree that life for each of them has been a failure. 'They die together.' "[26]

II

As an orphan "run through the world," Huck would seem to share the archetypal condition of many other fictional protagonists who, especially in the nineteenth century, tell their histories in order to claim their lives. But this assertion of identity, which depends upon the interplay of self-knowledge and social experience, is, as we have seen, short-circuited by the strategy of the ending. The significance of this pattern for American self-imagery becomes even clearer when we contrast Huck's narrative with that of his nearest European cousin, Pip, the hero of Dickens's *Great Expectations*.

To summarize the parallels between these histories: each is centered on the relation of a fatherless boy to parental figures whose moral qualities (virtues as well as failings) indict the character and/or the social institutions of an entire society. Both boys fear and distrust the operations of the adult world and have received first-hand instruction in its cruelties. For each, society is a prison, his own conscience the jailer. Each suffers an exacerbated sense of guilt in which intuitive moral impulses vie with an over-mastering sense of sinfulness enforced through social conditioning. For each, the burden of guilt (temporarily or permanently, as their differing outcomes will show) blocks growth toward adult identity. Yet the structure of the books and the resolution toward which they carry their protagonists suggest a striking contrast in the versions of self-definition which each culture supports.[27]

Pip's history, like Huck's, begins with his submission to the strictures of a socially imposed conscience. Just as Huck has been goaded by the Widow and Miss Watson to distrust every natural impulse and reaction, so Pip, stealing food and a file for Magwitch, believes himself to be as great a criminal as the poor brute starving out on the marshes. The horrors of Magwitch's condition, the hunger, loneliness and rage that complement his criminal state, are ironically counterpointed in the Christmas meal at the Gargerys'. With his chest squeezed against a corner of the table, Pip, accounted to be "naturally wicious" by the hypocrite Pumble-chook, is fed scraps and leavings from the Christmas pig, because he, unlike the pig, shows little promise of productive value (a prophecy which will be brought to ironic fulfillment in Pip's sub-sequent life as an indolent and enviable 'gentleman'). Here, the eating anxieties associated with childhood, in which nourishment and love are conjoined, not only dramatize the emotional impover-ishment of Pip's world but, by figurative extension, the heart-lessness of the larger world in which Magwitch suffers. The identification between the boy and the criminal, with its implicit conflation of familial and social cruelty, is brought full circle when Magwitch later tells Pip that he first became aware of himself thieving turnips for a living: "Summon had run away from me – a man – a tinker – and he'd took the fire with him and left me wery cold."[28]

Like Jim, Magwitch, who is also in chains, expresses through his own body the harsh and punitive nature of life in the body politic. But Pip's reaction to him (and subsequently to Joe) sets the English boy on a very different course from that which Huck pursues. Magwitch is a grotesque image of the rage and violence Pip fears and will repress in himself, and whose shadow will then begin to dog him in Orlick, the wolf-hearted criminal, his hand turned against the world. The natural anger that we might expect from Pip toward those who revile and exploit him – from his sister and Pumblechook to Miss Havisham and Estella – is, instead, internalized as a revulsion from everything coarse and common in himself and his surroundings. Pip's snobbery thus points up the association between class aspiration and psychic repression, and it suggests not only the cost to the self of survival in English society, but also the mechanism by which that society defends itself against an awareness of the suffering of its victims. Until Pip is brought face-to-face with the man whose work has supported him and who considers him a son, he is perfectly willing to be supported and to accept his money on the condition that he ask nothing about where it comes from or what struggles and intentions it represents.

Just as Pip rejects all memory of his material benefactor, so he manages to evade all compunction toward his moral one – Joe, the loving parent, who provides him with examples of what selflessness means. Between them, Magwitch and Joe divide many of the qualities that are united in Huck's Jim, and in both books the parental figures are primitives, their nature and experience seemingly irrelevant to the dominant structure of their societies. But while Jim (and Pap Finn) remain unchanged throughout *Huckleberry Finn* (both in themselves and in their relation to the larger social order), the parental figures in *Great Expectations* not only grow as moral beings, but become to some degree acculturated in the course of the story. Their developing literacy is emblematic of their potential as a source of well-being for the precarious health of English middle-class society.

Pip's callousness toward his kindly but impotent 'father,' as well as his repression of the memory of the violent Magwitch, might be likened to Huck's ability either to forget Jim or to distance himself from the impact of Jim's condition whenever he is on shore. But Pip, after rejecting both negative and positive aspects of these parental figures, comes to recognize the strength of his ties to both. Given their role in his early life, and the reminders of their presence which continue to haunt him, it is clear that his reconciliations are as much with aspects of his own nature as they are with Joe and Magwitch themselves.

Huck, on the other hand, never achieves this fusion with split-off or rejected parts of himself. His relation to Jim, as well as to his real father and his life on the shore, is figured in a series of metaphoric rebirths, each of which enables him to slough off a previous identity without troubling over its emotional consequences. So when Huck stages his death for Pap Finn and is reborn to a life with Jim, Pap disappears from both Huck's consciousness and ours. Jim becomes the loving, nurturing parent he has needed all along. When Pap's "people" (or doubles) turn up in the shape of the duke and king, they are only obstacles that Huck must learn to manipulate or circumvent, in the same way that he maneuvers through events on shore. Pap, with his "fish-belly" white face, represents an evil threat which Huck evades through symbolic self-murder, not a force in himself with which he must come to terms. To adapt Sartre's phrase, Huck has learned very early that "Hell is *other* people" [my italics]. It is this attitude that controls the outcome of all his relationships – even that with Jim. For as Jim rejoins society, accepting his forty dollars and his manumission, he merges into that "sivilized" background which enables Huck to forget him too, to turn him into a merely decent, and ultimately featureless shore 'darky.'

The winding-up of Huck's affairs on shore – simultaneously paying off Jim and learning from him that Pap is dead – is a way not only of simplifying and dismissing Huck's obligations within the social order, but any possibility of a personal life of his own. Huck need feel no more guilt over his responsibility to Jim, and no more fear of Pap. While Pip's journey enmeshes him more deeply in a web of authentic human relations, through which he comes to know himself, Huck opts for a vision of freedom which essentially protects him from those conflicted feelings of right and wrong, that struggle between social and personal loyalties and values through which true individuality is defined.

None of the characters in *Huckleberry Finn* really changes in the process of time. Indeed, time as an element hardly exists in the story. The book's medium is space. The raft drifts along in the flow of the river, carrying its occupants from one town to another. In this world rebirth is an apt metaphor, because there are no apparent connections between dramatic events. Characters emerge and disappear with the passing scenery along the riverbank. Huck's own memory, the interiority of his associations and thoughts, which would provide a sense of temporal continuity, is absent for large portions of the story. Only in the exaggerated artifice of the ending – with the reappearance of Tom and Sid Sawyer and Aunt Polly – is there a connection to figures from Huck's past.

By contrast, *Great Expectations* is filled with recurring relationships. Mr Jaggers, Herbert Pocket, Miss Havisham, Estella – virtually everyone that Pip has met in the first part of his life plays a role in his London years. And not only do they affect Pip, but each has a personal history which reveals the pressure that the past exerts on present events. This sense of time, rather than space, as the determinant of character, with both imprisoning and liberating potential, expresses faith in a relatively stable social order. In this regard, the world of *Huckleberry Finn*, predicated on Huck's fear of entangling alliances, is closer to that of Moll Flanders – with her uncanny ability to forget husbands and children in her concentration on survival – than to the more consistent temporality of the conventional British nineteenth-century novel. For though we know that Mark Twain wrestled with the question of how character is shaped, his fiction seems designed as a reaction to rather than an exploration of this issue.[29]

But for Dickens's hero, from his earliest forays among family tombstones, it is the unquestioning acceptance of a fully-socialized sense of existence that defines the shape of identity. When the Widow's dismal and devout ways get to be too much for him, Huck lights out, puts on his old rags and climbs into a hogshead; while Pip, "brung up" under the hard hand of his shrewish sister, turns to Joe for secret comfort or simply goes up to his attic room and cries. It is understood that with or without Miss Havisham's money, Pip will be bound in apprenticeship to Joe – and the social metaphor implied in the action of hands which bind, control, exploit, but may ultimately redeem others resonates throughout the book.

For Pip to break loose from what Edmund Wilson called "imprisoning states of mind" means to transmute not to escape the nature of one's bonds with others.[30] Though Pip, like Huck, has an abiding sense of the loneliness and isolation at the heart of the human condition, society offers him the only possible refuge – the saving grace of human warmth. For Huck, however, loneliness is more intolerable within the constrictions of the social order than outside it. It is on the shore that he is haunted by images of death, that he fears ghosts, and feels a complementary emptiness inside himself, whereas loneliness on the river never produces this degree of anxiety. Compare, for example, Huck on Jackson's Island with Pip's imagining of Magwitch alone on the marshes.

When it was dark I set by my camp fire smoking, and feeling pretty satisfied; but by-and-by it got sort of lonesome, and so I went and set on the bank and listened to the currents washing along, and counted the stars . . . and then went to bed; there ain't no better way to put in time when you are lonesome; you can't stay so, you soon get over it.   (p. 34)

And here is Pip looking out of the blacksmith's window:

It was a dry, cold night, and the wind blew keenly, and the frost was white and hard. A man would die to-night of lying out on the marshes, I thought. And then, I looked at the stars, and considered how awful it would be for a man to turn his face up to them as he froze to death, and see no help or pity in all the glaring multitude.
                                                                                       (p. 80)

So in resolving to quit England and the life he has known, in order to accompany Magwitch in his escape abroad, Pip is able to come to terms with the buried emotions of his own past. The death struggle with Orlick, who accuses Pip of murdering his own sister ("Wolf," said he . . . "Old Orlick's a going to tell you somethink. It was you as did for your shrew sister. . . . I tell you it was done through you" [p. 437]), however artificially contrived, makes clear that the hidden root of Pip's guilt lies in his violently rebellious childhood feelings toward his sister. Through a kind of trial by combat, Pip, in effect, triumphs over the criminal in himself. Freed of this weight, he is free of his identification with and horror of Magwitch the outlaw. Instead, he can respond to the old man's humanity and thus find his own.

In his final actions, Pip's energies redeem not only Magwitch's last days, but also Miss Havisham's, and they affect Estella's character as well. Ultimately, Pip finds enough decency and good for him to take his place in the world as it is. In contrast, Huck's struggle with himself to free Jim involves coming to terms with few social or personal demons: it is brief, just, and ultimately irrelevant to the outcome of the narrative. As Huck is enabled to evade his violent feelings toward his father, so he never gets the chance to risk his life either for a moral principle or a personal obligation. He never comes to grips with the central moral issue that the book proposes: Jim's enslavement is also his enslavement. The mode of thinking that accepts slavery as normal and even considers Jim ungrateful for not being more thankful to Miss Watson for her care of him will accept any received opinion as truth once it has been socially confirmed. Huck's action consists not in risking himself by a challenge to this kind of thought but in fleeing it. The net effect is that he never grows up, never faces the consequences of fighting for the value of his own thoughts and feelings, never experiences that sense of full reawakening which signifies Pip's initiation into maturity.

As I looked along the clustered roofs, with Church towers and spires shooting into the unusually clean air, the sun rose up, and a veil seemed to be drawn from the river, and millions of sparkles burst out of its waters. From me too, a veil seemed to be drawn, and I felt strong and well. (p. 444)

Like Mark Twain's novel, Dickens's too has its own kind of double ending, but this does not lie in the essentially irrelevant question of whether Pip gets Estella. It is rather, the bifurcation between what Barbara Hardy calls Pip's "moral success" and the limited, rather bleak social condition that he accepts for himself.[31] For Magwitch and Pip can no more be allowed to escape to Holland and start life over than could Huck and Jim be imagined as settling into neighborly relations in the American South, or any-where else, for that matter. In neither book do individual relations have the power to triumph over the inhumanity of the larger social world. But while Huck flees this world, Pip finds a middle station in it that allows him to practice the old virtues of modesty, decency, and personal charity, for a while. It is significant that he finds such a situation, not in London, where his expectations have gone to ruin, but in a colonial outpost. The failure of these expectations thus comes to stand for the social failure of Victorian society, whose economic optimism has only resulted in newer forms of social heartlessness.[32]

What Pip settles for is a kind of nostalgia for the future – a hope that an earlier and more decent version of mercantile capitalism might still prosper at some distance from the fierce, industrial, imperial center. However, a ship-broker in Cairo, or any such position in the suburbs of empire, raises more social issues than it resolves. What Dickens's final disposition does is to align the bounds of moral experience with the limitations of human history – an arrangement Mark Twain could only conceptualize as an ironic dream.

For having insisted that authenticity between human beings can only be envisaged outside social boundaries, Mark Twain becomes increasingly uncertain as to where one locates reality – which dream is the real fiction? Though there has been much effort to account for his later pessimistic despair in biographical terms, it is worth noting that his preoccupation with the confusions between reality and dream were not only shared by the Melville of both *Moby-Dick* and *Pierre*, but were a fascination as well as an eventual torment to Hawthorne in his late romances.[33] There are other American writers and thinkers one might enlist in this company; the point is made only to suggest that this preoccupation may be exacerbated by that particular combination of visionary idealism and social despair which American moral ambition tends to encourage.

4

Strether Unbound: The Selective Vision of Henry James's Ambassador

And the wasting of life is the implication of death.   *Notebooks*

At the close of this elegiac novel, whose theme of the unlived life seemed to haunt James throughout his own,[1] Lambert Strether cuts his last tie to his Paris adventure by extricating himself from the spell of Maria Gostrey's domestic warmth. Sitting at her breakfast table with his eye on a "ripe round melon," he announces that he is not "in real harmony with what surrounds me."[2] Since Miss Gostrey has just offered to make her home a "haven of rest" for him, the comment, at the least, might be taken as a gentleman's excuse for rejecting what amounts to a lady's marriage proposal. Indeed, James says in the preface that he never had any intention of allowing Strether to take the invitation seriously. Rather, he wanted this scene "to express as vividly as possible certain things quite other than itself"[3] – and so it does. For, on a deeper level of meaning, Strether's rejection of Miss Gostrey's offer completes our sense of the very "mould" of the New Englander's consciousness – those things of "fixed and appointed measure"[4] in his nature which are now seen to define him and to determine his peculiar destiny.

Strether claims that he must leave Paris in order "to be right." "Not, out of the whole affair, to have got anything for myself" (p. 344). "It's you who would make me wrong!" he tells Miss Gostrey. Yet whatever is "fixed" in Strether's nature is not made perfectly clear. There is enough ambiguity in these phrases to have divided readers in their judgment of just where Strether does come out, and therefore what, if anything, he has gained from his experience. Has he achieved a self-knowledge that implies acceptance of his limitations? Or is his insistence on being "right" a reversion to the self-righteousness of Woollett? Is his moral scrupulousness a form of integrity? Or is it based on nothing more than vanity and false pride: how he would be judged by others – Mrs

Newsome, in particular – if he stayed? Does his insistence on an absolute morality mask a deeper fear of life, having been forced to see it 'closeup' in Marie de Vionnet's demeaning passion for Chad? Or has her passion educated him to "life's vastness and diversity"? One could go on with the putative causes for Strether's retreat – perhaps he is merely a disappointed lover, having been strongly attracted to Madame de Vionnet himself.[5] Each of these possibilities can be educed from the complex texture of Strether's psychology; each adds a stroke to James's portrait of the "poor gentleman" whose sensibility and powers of appreciation are finer than the provincial objects on which, heretofore, they have been exercised.

At bottom, the conflict in these views turns upon whether one thinks Strether's renunciation redeems or destroys him, and, to a lesser extent, whether this outcome reflects a conscious or less than conscious intention on James's part. To note this is to realize that these arguments are essentially irresolvable, because the greater their persuasiveness the more inevitably they reflect extra-textual values and insights, as indeed my own judgments do. Yet, however one evaluates the cost and meaning of Strether's final decision, it seems to me that James provides ample narrative evidence to support the idea that Strether has achieved, on his own terms, the integrity of a private vision.

Strether is a determinist who voices about himself the same delimiting view of the conditions that have made him that James expresses in the preface quoted above.

What one loses one loses; make no mistake about that. The affair – I mean the affair of life – couldn't no doubt have been different for me; for it's at best a tin mould . . . into which, a helpless jelly, one's consciousness is poured. (p. 132)

Determinism may be a self-fulfilling prophecy, but Strether's limitations as well as his ambitions provide a compelling example of its effects. For despite his romantic pulsations, Strether is tied to the culture which has bred him; his strengths and principles, prejudices and fears are all shown to be inherent in the now-desiccated spiritual soil of late nineteenth-century New England. So at the last, mildly but firmly, he reverts to something old but still operative in his nature and heritage. Rejecting all compromise and accommodation with the world for the authority of a personal vision of integrity, he arrives at a state of inner freedom that leaves him attached to nothing at all but the memory of his "wonderful impressions." The cause of Strether's resistance to things as they are may be enfolded in ambiguities, but the effect, I believe, is not. At the end of the story we are clearly encouraged to feel that Strether has achieved his own version of manhood.

Throughout the narrative, Strether's vulnerability to feelings of embarrassment, even shame, at his misjudgment of European social and moral codes has lent substance to the metaphor by which he characterizes his relationship to Miss Gostrey. He sees himself first as an infant, then a toddler, holding on to the hem of her garment as she leads him through the byways of experience. But in the final scene between them their positions are reversed. Though he may not be at home, he is master of their encounter.[6] It is she who now looks up to him, announcing "I can't indeed resist you," even though the definition of integrity he offers puts him at odds with both Woollett and Paris, and, therefore, with her. At fifty-five Strether has completed his initiation: he has grown up not to enter the world more fully, but rather to leave it more certainly behind.

Strether's alternative to the civilized comforts of Miss Gostrey's hearth is the prospect of a bleak self-sufficiency in the place he knows best. Reality itself has turned out to be the cheat. Paris ends by disappointing him as much as Woollett. His return to America will be to "a great difference" in which Mrs Newsome, the unseen Other in his life will no longer figure either. Strether, like the hero of Emerson's "Nature," having assimilated the lessons of all his "friends," finds that their "office is closing"; that they are no longer coextensive with his needs.[7] At the end of this novel, then, Strether achieves a traditional American version of self-reliance. His choice is either to submit to a world whose conventions and values (American and European) he finds do not agree with his spiritual stomach, or to save himself by asserting his own integrity, not as "mere antinomianism" but as the ideal alternative to all lesser and warring parts.[8] Like the other protagonists whose journeys we have traced, there is no middle ground for Strether between his own version of moral idealism and the complexities, compromises, and half-truths he has found, even in the world he most prizes. His gain from experience is comprised in an inner vision – an ideal merger of aesthetic and moral meaning whose conditions life itself utterly denies.

77

In response to Miss Gostrey's question whether Chad may already have another woman in London, Strether replies: "Yes. No. That is I *have* no ideas. I'm afraid of them. I've done with them" (p. 344). At the end of this novel there are many things that Strether is done with. For he saves himself at the cost of an extraordinary self-restriction. Although his experience has been often interpreted as an example of the growth of an artist's consciousness, Strether is not an artificer. Like little Bilham, he lacks the power to give original form to experience.[9] His vision does not drive him toward that "reality of experience" which, for instance, Stephen Dedalus goes forward to meet at the end of *A Portrait of the Artist as a Young Man*. For 'seeing,' which at the novel's opening had been anticipated by Strether as the key to boundless freedom, has at the close become entirely a matter of memory. The warm circle of life to which Strether had earlier responded in Miss Gostrey's home has been transmuted into a collection of "wonderful impressions," those germs of consciousness which will serve as "his loaf on the shelf" for the bleak days ahead. Recollection is to be his only mode of participation.

If Strether ends in a desert of the ideal, committed to nothing but the savoring of his impressions, he begins with a directly antithetical hope. Reversing the spiritual geography of western myth, this inner alien from Woollett, Massachusetts, conceives of his arrival in Europe as an entry into a new world, whose treasure of moral and aesthetic possibilities promises release from the crippling categorical judgments of his American past. From the first, Strether is presented to us as a man "in the middest,"[10] whose errand, in its largest sense, is to close with the world, to make sense of himself (and therefore of it) from where he stands. A widower in the late middle years of his life, he is haunted by the failure of his youthful aspirations and the betrayal of his deepest human tie. For the spontaneity and warmth of personal relations, he has substituted the constraints of duty and conscience – what James in *The Notebooks* calls "pure appearance and daily tasks." Burdened by a nameless anxiety that keeps him obsessed "with the other thing" (p. 26), he is unable to locate himself in the moment, to meet the eyes of his companion. Like the breached and ancient city wall of Chester around which he and Miss Gostrey take their first walk together, Strether is a kind of ruined fortress of the American moral sense. So his plea to Miss Gostrey to "get me out" (p. 26) represents the first stirrings of a rebellion against the encircling conditions of his life.

The challenge of Europe for Strether – which serves emblematically as the scene of the world ("a massive aggregate of experiential possibilities"[11]) lies in the opening it gives him to sift between true and false values, to exchange the given stereotypes of a publicly sanctioned "conscience" for the hard-won truths of his own perception of reality. At first glance this would seem to be merely another version of the age-old psychic task of adolescence. What makes Strether's case arresting is both his advanced age and the way it figures in the larger pattern of his representative status. For like his country, Strether has his youth behind him and feels it somehow to have been betrayed; that he had lost or surrendered it before he could fully understand its purpose. For Strether, youth is associated with freedom and freedom, significantly, with the unsealing of his eyes as he watches "the first swallows of the year weaving their flight" around the cathedral tower above him. Miss Gostrey (whom James designates as the reader's friend) diagnoses his trouble as the general American "failure to enjoy" (p. 25).

However, Strether's renewed capacity to enjoy leads not to the ideal image of social and personal felicity as he comes to imagine it in this "new world," but to the recognition that in deepening the possibilities for feeling and expression, the traditions and conventions of old societies also impose a terrible cost. What Strether discovers is that there is no freedom from the commonplace "vulgarities" of human existence; no transcendence in experience from its given conditions because the personal relations that sustain us have a passional core that is inseparable from a sense of pain and victimization – especially acute for those like Madame de Vionnet, who, in representing civilization's finest effects, are most entrapped by its realities.

Strether's initiation into this world proceeds by stages in which he is torn between the claims of his Woollett conscience – embodied in the conventional moral views and purposes of Mrs Newsome – and his deepening attraction to the individual illuminations of consciousness which Paris, and especially Madame de Vionnet, seem to offer. In this story James plays the popular image of Paris as a Babylon of pleasure – what in *The Notebooks* he calls "the banal side of the revelation of Paris"[12] – against its historic value as an icon of the aesthetic achievements of Western culture; indeed, of the aesthetics of Western history itself, in which, for Strether, nobility and cruelty, beauty and vulgarity shimmer against each other like the glinting facets of a jewel. It is just this confusion of boundaries and categories – of sensuous surface with what may or may not be underlying moral squalor – that generates in Strether's conflicted Protestant soul a sense of pleasurable bewilderment. He wonders if it is possible "to like Paris enough without liking it too much" (p. 65). Paradoxically, the uncertainty and misapprehension which ensue free him to envision a finer relation between personality and its social environment than any he has known. Paris thus serves him as a kind of moral wilderness, a place of transition which becomes "a realm of pure possibility,"[13] stimulating him to new aspirations and more subtle discriminations.

For much of the story, Strether is encouraged to believe that the social particulars of Parisian life, with Madame de Vionnet at its radiant center, are consonant with his own powers of perception; that what nurtures him aesthetically has – in the manifest transformation of Chad by this "wonderful woman" – its moral complement in the behavior of others. So his experience seems to him an almost magical boon, a gift of vision after a long dry season that allows him to enter vicariously into those possibilities of the fully-expressed life which had once before filled him with hope when, as a young man, he had brought his bride to Paris on their wedding trip. Thus he explains to Miss Gostrey the value he places on his relation to Chad and the Countess:

"The point is that they're mine. Yes, they're my youth, since somehow at the right time nothing ever was. What I meant just now therefore is that it would all go – go before doing its work – if they were to fail me." (p. 197)

Given the quality of Strether's consciousness, his sense of youth is no simple matter of energy and high spirits alone. It is a retrospective youth that he experiences – one that infuses Chad's physical vitality, taste and ease of bearing with the shaping power of Madame de Vionnet's wisdom, grace, and surpassing beauty. Together, the couple exemplify for Strether a kind of living aesthetic, a unique instance of that freedom to enact life's highest possibilities that he recommends to little Bilham ("Live all you can; it's a mistake not to" [p. 132]). For Strether, as for little Bilham, what counts in this statement is not the meaningless flux of experience itself, but its translation into the data of impressions, those perceptions of consciousness which are the marks of his increasingly revivified and expanded sensibility.

In his transports of pleasure at the sight of Chad with innocent little Jeanne de Vionnet, his recognition that "it was that rare youth he should have enjoyed being 'like' " (p. 133), as well as his acute happiness at the color and texture of his surroundings – the straw-colored Chablis, the *omelette aux tomates,* the grey eyes of Marie de Vionnet – Strether provides a particularly American turn on Pater's description of the model critic. In *The Renaissance*,[14] Pater speaks of the aesthetic critic in terms with which Lambert Strether would no doubt be familiar, as an elder of Wollett's cultural élite. The "aim of the true student of aesthetics" is to multiply sensations, "curiously testing new opinions and courting new impressions" from all forms of life – whether a song, a picture or "an engaging personality." This is the first step, says Pater, in seeing "the object in itself as it really is,"[15] for to experience impressions strongly "one must realize such primary data for oneself, or not at all."

But no sooner are Strether's eyes open to seeing "the object as in itself it really is" – possibilities that for him are prized for the sense of personal rebirth they afford – than he is faced with those bewildering epistemological questions that Pater insistently discounts. For Pater says that to experience "impressions strongly," to discriminate between them, to analyze their effect on oneself is enough. There is no need to trouble over futile metaphysical questions of "what beauty is in itself, or what its exact relation to truth and experience" may be.[16] But these are the very questions that Strether, steeped in the New England tradition of the moral, not the aesthetic, responsibility of the individual perceiver, cannot ultimately ignore. To see the object in itself is, for him, to be reminded of certain discounted moral values in the world toward which he is drawn. Ultimately, for Strether, to see the object in itself means to face up to the question of the relation between its moral and aesthetic nature. For the ideal that he seeks is precisely a conjunction of these two realms of value. This is the question that he both pursues and evades throughout his Parisian adventure. Do people show "for what they really are?" he prods Miss Barrace (p. 126). "Judge for yourself," responds little Bilham, who has just remarked to him that "You're not a person to whom it's easy to tell things you don't want to know" (p. 123).

As Strether proceeds, it becomes apparent that dualism as such, whatever its content, represents the structuring principle of his consciousness. For what begins in his mind as a contrast between American and European ways of taking experience – a comedy of manners versus morals, age versus youth, innocence versus experience – metamorphoses as it deepens to reveal an irremediable tension at the center of his nature: the more he strives to overcome his dualism in a visionary ideal, the more he is haunted by the antithetical sense of a harsh reality which will inevitably destroy it.

The standard critical view of the opposition in Strether's mind defines it in terms of "two equally desirable yet mutually exclusive possibilities for life" embodied in the settings of Europe and America, which are either dialectically transcended in Strether's action at the end or mutually destroyed.[17] But while it is eminently clear, through the notation of his own thoughts, that the opposition of aesthetics and morals forms the central figure in Strether's divided consciousness, this construction taken alone seems to me to simplify the drama of his character. For he is never the objective or impartial judge of competing possibilities that these abstractions imply. From the moment he lands in England, Strether is "hit." All his imaginative energy runs toward the mysteries and possibilities of the one shore, while its backwash of fear and anxiety draws him toward the safety of the other. To divorce Strether from the emotional content of his experience – his desire to "believe" despite doubt – and the coloration this brings to his conflicting values, is to deny the novel its measure of felt life and to reduce it to a mere tract or blueprint for James's ideas. Rather than thinking of Strether as arbitrating or vacillating between "equally desirable yet mutually exclusive possibilities for life," I find it more convincing to define his central tension (and that of the narrative) as a search for an ideal yet worldly form that unites aesthetic and moral realms of being, but which is always under threat from an opposing inner reality whose "messages" insist that an ocean of distance inevitably separates these two.[18]

Moreover, this central opposition between ideal and real has its subdivisions within both the 'American' and 'European' scenes of his consciousness. Just as Strether's initial prejudice about Chad's "woman" reflects a harsh and narrow American moral reality, later embodied in the Pococks' errand, so his opposing moral idealism is based on sanctions for inner truth that look back to the first American errand and provide him with a standard for the authority of his own judgment. Conversely, the rigid social codes which define the rules of everyday existence in Europe hint to Strether of a coldness and duplicity at the core of high civilization that all the idealized beauty of its appearances cannot mask. Strether is indeed a multiply divided man whose consciousness, for all its play with nuance and ambiguity, finally reflects the "stress upon contending and irreconcilable opposites" inherent in his Calvinist tradition – an opposition which I believe the ending reifies rather than transcends or destroys.[19]

The fact that Strether's consciousness is both subject and object of the narrative – that, with one or two exceptions, what we see and know and feel about the world he sees, we see and know and feel about him as well – allows us to recognize that his misperceptions of the world around him are essentially self-deceptions. For Strether never functions merely as an innocent or ignorant transmitter of impressions he doesn't understand. He is far too clever and discriminating an observer to be simply the guileless fool he often takes himself for. Rather, little Bilham hits the mark when he tells Strether that what the elder man doesn't know, he doesn't wish to know. Perhaps this is because what Strether most fears to see is the destruction of an illusion which he already knows is just that.[20] Psychologically speaking, his naiveté might be conceived as an unconscious blindfold that protects inner vision from the assaulting sight of complex truth. What the narrator says early in the book about Maria Gostrey's wish not to know the facts of the Woollett product that provides Chad's income, applies with equal force to Strether. "In ignorance she could humor her fancy, and that proved a useful freedom" (p. 48). Strether's determined ignorance provides him with just such a pragmatic tool. Thus his description of the "virtuous attachment" is articulated with his head cast back, his eyes on the ceiling, lost, as the narrator says, "in the vision of it" (p. 168). To little Bilham, Strether confides: "It's a friendship, of a beautiful sort; and that's what makes them so strong . . . they keep each other up . . . she keeps the whole thing up . . . however, as a mere man, he may sometimes rebel. . . . She has simply given him an immense moral life, and what that can explain is prodigious" (p. 168). Once having worked out the dynamics of this "script" Strether holds to it as the fixed center of his imaginary universe despite all intimations to the contrary.

It is significant, therefore, that when he learns of Sarah Pocock's imminent arrival, its effect is to make him "afraid of himself" (p. 201). As the avatar of her mother "he already felt [Sarah] . . . come down on him, already burned, under her reprobation with the blush of guilt, already consented by way of penance, to the instant forfeiture of everything." The imagery here suggests the sinful feelings of a naughty child about to be shamed by a punitive and self-righteous parent – and Sarah Pocock is designedly the most distasteful character in the book. She is said to be far worse than her mother, "unpleasant" where Mrs Newsome is "mercifully vague" (p. 208). "Mother's worth fifty of Sally!" says Chad (p. 203).

But if all this is true, why does Strether accord the new ambassador this power over him? Why does the mere contemplation of her make him feel ready to scourge himself? His deepest worry is that the Pococks' blindness to Chad's transformation might show him (Strether) to have been living "in a false world," now menaced "by the touch of the real" (p. 212); in other words, that his perceptions, the ground of his newborn identity, are in peril of being swept away by a chill blast of New England moral "reality." It seems clear from the acuteness of Strether's reaction that the vision which he projects onto Chad and Madame de Vionnet (who do their part to encourage it) represents the goal of his own desire to transcend the iron conditions of his inner life, the "mould" from which his own consciousness inevitably takes its form (p. 132). In this sense, Sarah and her mother are ghosts of his own divided nature.

For it is just when Strether begins to suspect the impending break with the actual Mrs Newsome, when her letters cease, that he feels most intensely the pressure of her presence within him. It strikes him that he "had never so lived with her as during this period of her silence." Her soundlessness allows him to envision her in the purity of her ideals. He is able to separate her intrinsic nature ("deep devoted delicate noble" [p. 195]) from Woollett's vulgar estimate of her appearance as "cold." In short, the "lady of Woollett" may withdraw her patronage, but this threat only drives her spirit more deeply into Strether's consciousness, where high-minded purity and moral righteousness continue to exert their pull.

However, Strether's break with the actual Mrs Newsome does

deepen his separation from one aspect of the reality she embodies, leaving him more than ever alone with his vision of the ideal. For in losing Mrs Newsome's patronage, Strether turns decisively away from that pragmatic alliance of business and culture which has supported him thus far. The morally ambitious "tributes to the ideal" which Mrs Newsome goes in for, and that serve as expiation for her wealth, are financed by production of "the unmentionable object" – a domestic item which has been built into the booming trade she inherited from her buccaneer progenitors. Strether's chance for a cushioned, protected existence is now to be tied to his marriage with the woman whose business keeps his name on the cover of Woollett's *Review*, and so provides him with his "one presentable scrap of identity" (p. 51). It is this burden of moral compromise, in all its implications, that he carries across the threshold of Europe, and from which he initially begs Miss Gostrey to get him out.

Strether's very mildness and passivity (as well as his initial exhaustion) might be conceived as the mask for a hidden rage not unlike that expressed by the Emerson of 'Self-Reliance' who proclaimed that "society everywhere is in conspiracy against the manhood of everyone of its members! It demands the surrender of liberty and cuture. The virtue in most request is conformity. Self-reliance is its aversion."[21]

But there is a deep irony in the progress of events that follow from Strether's declaration of independence from Mrs Newsome, for if he remained true to the goals which his criticism of her implies, the reader would be justified in believing that he had truly achieved a spiritual renewal.[22] What Strether comes to see and reject in Mrs Newsome is her need to impose a fixed moral scheme on circumstances which resist her *a priori* categories. He finds that Woollett's view of her turns out, after all, to be his. She is "all . . . fine cold thought." Though a devotee of culture, she is blind to its highest manifestations – the possibilities to which Strether has tried to convert her, writing her long confessional notes on blue paper in order to make her see what he sees. Mrs Newsome has her own sense of what exaltation dictates; her response has been to assert the primacy of her own view over his reports. Strether acknowledges that she has a certain vision, but it is not his because "there's no room left; no margin . . . for any alteration in her scheme" (p. 298).

But like Oedipus condemning himself out of his own mouth, Strether accuses Mrs Newsome of precisely the moral rigidity and *a priori* certainty that he is about to display toward Madame de Vionnet. And, ironically, the solution to his problem with Mrs Newsome, which he admits he is unable to implement fully, is just the one that he does enact toward Madame de Vionnet. In reference to the lady of Woollett, he tells Miss Gostrey:

"What it comes to . . . is that you've morally and intellectually to get rid of her."
"Which would appear to be practically what you've done."
"I haven't touched her. She won't be touched." (p. 298)

Unlike Madame de Vionnet who seems to dissolve with Strether's rejection of her, Mrs Newsome remains dangerously intact in his imagination, like a "large iceberg in a cool blue northern sea" (p. 298).

Ultimately, what binds Strether to Mrs Newsome and makes his struggle against the "mould" of his moral nature so futile is that he, like her other American ambassadors, cannot accept the European view that moral codes may be different for different classes, or circumstances, or categories of experience. The most obvious distinction is the one Madame de Vionnet herself points out to Strether when she says that she and Chad cannot go about in public together. Though the Countess lives publicly apart from her husband, she must still observe all the proprieties of a married woman. But in private, among friends and acquaintances, she and Chad are a perfectly acceptable couple. It is even correct for this "friend" to arrange the marriage of her own daughter – who tries obediently to please her mother in this, as in all matters pertaining to their mutual interests. This combination of acute docility to public forms and extraordinary license in private acts is as repugnant to Strether, when he is eventually forced to acknowledge its reality, as it is to the Pococks. But while for the latter public propriety ought to dictate the standards of private morality, for Strether the case is just the reverse. Public morality ought to emanate from the highest personal standards, but there must be no discrepancy, no fiction or lie, between what shows forth and what truly is. While Strether's moral scheme represents the marriage of a cultural and a spiritual ideal, Sarah Pocock's represents its secular corruption. Nevertheless, in his final retreat from the complexities and ambiguities of human reality, it seems to me that

Strether's dream has a familial resemblance to Mrs Newsome's own.

Strether's response to Madame de Vionnet is therefore the crucial hinge on which this drama of consciousness turns. For his involvement with her, while it tests and reveals her possibilities, becomes the test of his own as well. What enlivens him as a character and gains our sympathy are just those persisting intuitions and doubts which flare up at the very moment he feels her charm most keenly. Although Madame de Vionnet seems to him on their first interview to be "one of the rare women he had so often heard of, read of, thought of, but never met" (p. 150), he also senses from the outset that she may use him, that "she'll try to make a fool of me." Stirred by her enormous personal appeal he vows "to save you if I can" (p. 152), but already feels himself in flight from her. The more he is drawn toward her, the more he struggles to escape. Conversely, every effort at distance brings him closer. As deeply as she appeals to something in his own nature, he fears the latent danger in her, for she is never just as she appears: "She was so odd a mixture of lucidity and mystery. . . . She spoke now as if her art were all an innocence, and then again as if her innocence were all an art" (p. 230). It is to Cleopatra that she is most often compared, first by Miss Barrace, then by Strether. She is said by Miss Barrace to be as various as fifty women, by Strether to take "all his categories by surprise" (p. 161). But the sense of complexity, fatality, and desperation evoked in this parallel lies dormant until Strether's final scene with her, when he leaves her to her predictably lonely fate.

It is fitting to the underlying pattern of an initiation story that Strether's fall into experience – the recognition which enables him to see that Madame de Vionnet is less sublime and more human than he had wished to believe – only occurs after he has cut his manifest ties to Mrs Newsome and feels himself most fully on his own and in possession of a new freedom. His thoughts of Madame de Vionnet are different too, as he muses on the recent change in the basis of their relationship – Chad has not been mentioned between them lately.

On this memorable day, when Strether goes into the countryside seeking the source of a French landscape painting he had once coveted but could not afford to buy from a Boston dealer, he has, ironically, never felt richer, never more master of his own composition. As his eye selects and arranges the scene before him, his memory occupies itself with the "theatre of his mind" – that metaphor for Strether's way of taking life which haunts the entire tale. But this harmony between inner and outer landscape (between a moral and aesthetic ideal) is abruptly shattered by the sudden appearance of Chad and Marie de Vionnet, "placing" themselves in his picture, with implications that he has been unwilling to conceive. Like Robin Molineux brought face to face with his trembling kinsman, Strether is forced to behold the profane side of that intimacy which he has for so long been pleased to consider only in terms of a pastoral idyll. The day closes with a sense of "violence averted" – a violence toward him which he feels as "quite horrible," as something in a dream.

At the supper they arrange to cover their mutual embarrassment, he conjures up images of dream, fiction, and fable to explain to himself what is happening. The more intensely Madame de Vionnet seeks to promote a fictitious version of her outing with Chad, the clearer it becomes to Strether that their relations all along have been dressed in a "lie." His pastoral, with its moral and aesthetic simplifications, has been shattered. The juxtaposition of Strether's ideal vision with this subsequent glimpse into moral duplicity reveals to him (and to us) the hopeless abyss between these differing realms of value; whatever else they may aspire to, human beings live primarily within the sphere of moral reality – and it is this truth, that of reality and its limitations, with which Strether must now come to terms.

James considered the final interview between Strether and Madame de Vionnet to be not only the climax of the novel, but "probably the most beautiful and interesting morsel in the book."[23] As food for thought it well repays close scrutiny, for it is in this scene that Strether loses forever the world he thought he had gained; and however he recasts it at the end, the price of this loss seems as much an impoverishment of himself as it is, in his eyes, of Madame de Vionnet.

Even before Strether faces the countess, he finds himself consciously reverting in thought to what the narrator calls "his old tradition . . . which even so many years of life had but little worn away" (p. 316). It is this New England tradition of moral rectitude which, indeed, makes it impossible, however he might let himself be charmed by her, to accept her actions with impunity. He cannot help feeling that someone must pay, that her happiness "presented some special difficulty" (p. 316). And though these evaluations subsequently dissolve under the force of her actual presence, their residue remains. Though Strether does not wish to judge her harshly, judge her he does.

Madame de Vionnet is never so compelling as when she appears to Strether in the simplicity of her suffering. Dressed in white, "as if for thunderous times" (p. 317), she suggests to him the image of Madame Roland on the scaffold. Nor is her pleading for Strether's support and friendship ever more moving than when she uses his own moral vocabulary ("selfish and vulgar") to condemn herself before him for the depth of her passion. But it is all to no avail. Strether can no longer ennoble her. All he can see is the moral humiliation to which her suffering leads. It is not a renovating freedom, as he had imagined, that is the governing principle of the beautiful life he has so admired in her, but its very opposite, a terrible victimization. As Stephen Donadio puts it: "Europe is finally seen to represent this world's things as an end in themselves . . . a limitation on one's identity and expectations."[24]

Just so, Strether's linking of Marie de Vionnet to Madame Roland suggests as much about his own response to her pleading as it does his prescience of how her relations with Chad will end. For Madame Roland has come down in history as a courageous liberal reformer sacrificed to a puritanical revolutionary ideal. Analogously, the aborted humanitarian possibilities which Marie de Vionnet represents are destroyed not by Chad's predictable inadequacies but by Strether's own intransigent resistance to what, in fact, established Madame de Vionnet's humanity most surely – her commonplace emotional and physical needs. It is Strether, finally, with his capacity for transcendentally pure discriminations, far more than Chad "the companion of mere earthly joys" (p. 322), who enacts the double role of judge and executioner when he denies Madame de Vionnet her last pathetic hope that he will stay near her (to champion her cause, or perhaps be there himself when Chad leaves). It is he who makes "an end" of her (p. 324).

What Strether never considers is that Madame de Vionnet's capacity for passion might indeed be the very source of her extraordinary qualities; that it is passion, generated from these human needs that issues in the sublime appearances which so beguile him. Lacking the true artist's sense of the dialectical relation between energy and form, the recognition of passion as the well-spring of life, Strether fails, for all his sensibility, to see very deeply or very steadily into the nature of the human condition. Madame de Vionnet's suffering confronts him with what he has never before allowed himself to imagine – the coercive force of sexual passion, the cruelty within the very sources of life.[25]

It is a cruelty whose effects Marie herself acknowledges when she observes (a few moments before Strether shuts the door on her) that her only certainty is that "I shall be the loser in the end" (p. 324). Earlier, Strether had sought for a "pretext of disgust" (p. 142) as a defense against his growing identification with Chad and attachment to her. He finds it here, in all that now seems to him degrading and repellent in her condition.

Pity her as he does, he cannot help but equate her crying with the vulgarity of a "maidservant." Despite all her subtlety, what he marvels at is that "a creature so fine, could be by mysterious forces, a creature so exploited" (p. 322). Indeed, he can hardly bear her as she is, sitting there before him: "It was actually moreover as if he didn't think of her at all, as if he could think of nothing but the passion, mature, abysmal, pitiful, she represented, and the possibilities she betrayed" (p. 323). What Strether finally manages to do in this scene is a variant of what he did with such ease in the "theatre of his mind" in the country: he abstracts from the intense reality of the woman before him those emotions and sensations he wishes to consider, while from Marie de Vionnet herself he withdraws.

To do more would be to respond to her empathetically, out of truly intimate human feeling. But Strether has had little experience of intimacy, and for empathy he would have to acknowledge a fallibility to match hers. For all his awareness of Madame de Vionnet's suffering, Strether never takes it for the mirror of his own.[26] He misses the opportunity to come to terms with his needs and limitations because, as Marie herself says, when "things become too ugly" (p. 324) he pulls up and flees. His moral imagination is finally a variant of Mrs Newsome's own. The "cool blue northern sea" remains intact.

The standard interpretation of the ending argues that Strether saves his life in this scene; that his use of the perfect tense to emphasize (both comically and brutally) the sense of injury as well as finality in his departure from Madame de Vionnet ("You've *had* me"), somehow frees him to experience the redeeming power of a wider, more inclusive consciousness.[27] It is, no doubt, testimony to James's success in eliciting the reader's cooperation in this protection of Strether, that those who support this reading most often fail to realize the cost it entails. For ultimately it requires one to concentrate exclusively on Strether's pain (as he does), and so tacitly to endorse his cruel rejection of Madame de Vionnet as the price of entry into a higher and seemingly more inclusive faith.

Moreover, that faith, if it is to be inclusive, surely must be based on Strether's own self-awareness; marked by some signal on Strether's part that would confirm our sense of him as a compassionate character, ready to acknowledge his own place in the human muddle. But it is just this evidence that is missing. Even though Strether is able to discriminate among values in a manner that sets him apart from many earlier American idealists, he no more than Emerson can be believed to have gained an all-inclusive consciousness by rejecting or discounting a central portion of human existence. For what nourishes consciousness, if not ordinary life?

In this scene, then, Strether comes to the end of his dream – and turns away from the human truths his experience provides. Instead, he saves himself from what seems to him to be utter destruction at the hands of the world by recasting his vision in a form that reverses its earlier terms. Possibility, which had formerly been associated with the widest prospects of human experience, is now entirely an affair of the mind – an inner vision that blends an ideally *exclusive* morality with a mental souvenir book of "wonderful impressions." Limitation, which had begun as the inner burden of a constricting provincial conscience, now denotes the deadly moral cruelties and betrayals of the world. The spheres of the real and ideal have exchanged places, but their isolation from one another is no longer a matter of symbolic geography, of an imaginative ambassadorial bridge between two mental continents. It is absolute.

Strether's vision thus seems a far more equivocal reward for what he has rejected than the standard celebratory descriptions of it imply. The sense of his impressions as "a loaf on the shelf" for the bleak days ahead is hardly commensurate with the notion of a "priceless" gift.[28] The loss is terrible because it emphasizes

Strether's impotence: he is unfit for both life and art. Perhaps, like the country, he has come to the end of his errand – the end of a spiritual adventure of renewal and rebirth which, again like the country, he refuses to relinquish and yet cannot truly regenerate through his own actions. He retreats instead into a retrospective dream of the world as it might have been, or as it ought to have been; a position that is at once self-protective and self-exalting. It makes of his experience a kind of ironic romantic spiral in which the failed ambitions of his youth return as a spiritualized memory of human perfection, while the common soil of human experience from which youth (and age) must actually nurture identity (and thereby consciousness) dissolves.

In the synopsis for *The Ambassadors*, Henry James says that if Strether had been an artist he would in some sense have lived, and this is why he did not make him one.[29] However, as the story proceeds, this negative *donnée*, which blocks the road to self-fulfillment in art, is multiplied as all roads to a connection or accommodation with human experience, with felt life, are blocked for Strether. In the characters of little Bilham, Waymarsh and Chad, James establishes three examples of what prove inevitably to be impossible versions of such accommodation. Each is a figure with whom Strether identifies a major aspect of his own nature – aesthetic, moral and material; each represents a way of taking life, of being in the world. But the structural parallels between Strether and each of them only underscore his ultimate distance from all.

Of the three, little Bilham's example is the most enticing. As an artist *manqué*, whose visual standards are too high for his own abilities, he has the capacity to realize what he is not, and the discriminating intelligence to value the world for what it can offer. There is nothing dualistic in Bilham's sensibility. He is perfectly in harmony with himself, and therefore with the world, in his chosen role of sympathetic observer. He has what Strether knows himself to lack, "moral ease." When Strether makes his singular attempt at self-revelation, admonishing little Bilham to live all he can while he is still young, to cultivate "the illusion of freedom" (p. 132), little Bilham redefines this comment, and in so doing provides Strether with the ironic terms of his own salvation. For the freedom which Strether has been associating with Chad and his own lost physical youth is subsequently reinterpreted by Bilham entirely in terms of aesthetic perception. "Live" fully equates with "see" ("*really* to see, for it must have been that only you meant" [p. 165]). It is thus the modest painter-man who shows Strether the way to repossess his youth – by transmuting the curse of a lost physical state into the blessing of a renewed spiritual one. But Bilham's very moral ease reveals his ultimate inadequacy as a model for Strether. Lacking the older man's moral idealism, he is perfectly ready to try to make himself marry Mamie Pocock if it will make Strether happy ("I'll do anything in the world for you!" [p. 259]). The cost of this extraordinary urbanity is a certain moral inconsequence; he is, perhaps, too much at home in the world. He lives for aesthetic pleasure, taking appearances and forms as they are without troubling over their history or their human price.

For Strether to follow little Bilham's way would be to remain in Paris near Miss Gostrey and submit himself to "the lust of the eyes and the pride of life" (p. 8), as he early calls her domain of beautiful things. But however seductive the pleasures of such a box in the theater of life, a "perched privacy," Strether turns his back on the spectacle.

Even less than little Bilham can the morose Waymarsh ("Milrose in person") be considered to offer a feasible pattern for moral accommodation. The men are united not only by their common heritage of the Puritan-Pilgrim past, but by a similar sense of *dis-ease* in the present. Waymarsh, an insomniac, is said to have barely escaped a nervous collapse by coming abroad; just as Strether was "pretty well run down" before he started (p. 31). "Prostration," connoting exhaustion, emptiness, even abasement, is the common keynote of their initial condition. In their separate ways each represents the etiolation of the old New England order – Puritan discipline without Puritan faith.

Waymarsh's appearance, a mix of strength, weakness, and fakery, is a virtual metaphor for the degeneration of American moral aspiration. Strether calls his face a ruined portrait, associating it with "the power and promise . . . of the American statesman . . . of an elder day" (p. 29). He has a "large handsome head" and a "great political brow"; but to hide the weak, slightly crooked lower half of the face, he has grown a beard. Waymarsh's increasing desperation finds outlet in his grim buying sprees – the sudden necessity that periodically overtakes him to rush into shops and purchase whatever his eye lights on. This plunge into the bog of what Waymarsh considers the wicked Old World is the reflux of what Strether calls his "sacred rage" – the old New England moral righteousness turned against itself. But, like his country, the spiritual emptiness of Waymarsh's moral categories leaves him open to exploitation on all sides. In Paris he falls into a kind of passive corruption. Allowing himself to be paraded like a trophy – a freak American celebrity – he is swept up in the giddy embrace of the clever Miss Barrace, who amuses herself with American "types." Promiscuously likening him to a Hebrew prophet or Indian chief, she fastens on the truth. He is simply an imposing cardboard outline.

All the while Waymarsh keeps an eye on Strether, worrying over his friend's apostasy and reporting back to Woollett about him. He is what Strether himself might have been without the grace of the latter's extraordinarily sensitive consciousness. It is part of the logic of his role as Strether's counterpart that he should shadow the latter in his central connection to the unseen Mrs Newsome. As Strether disengages and is displaced, Waymarsh grows more constant and captive to her. Finally, trapped by his own moral sterility, Waymarsh ends, rosy and benevolent, in the role of attendant to Sarah Pocock. Strether's last glimpse of him suggests a whited sepulcher. Waymarsh, dressed in a white summer waist-coat and wide panama looks now like a "Southern planter of the great days," his "sacred rage" – that last relic of moral autonomy – gone "feeble and flat" (pp. 268, 273).

Finally, there is Chad, the object of Strether's errand, whose return will not only secure Strether's marriage but enlarge its financial rewards. As Waymarsh bluntly puts it, if Strether gets Chad home, "he will marry more money" (p. 73). Yet even before he meets the prodigal son and has his prejudices confounded by what he sees, Strether begins to make a deep association between his own missed youth and Chad's rather frightening opportunities for "romantic privilege." Thus, from the start Chad is linked with both sides of Strether's material life – his Woollett gains and the new-found sensory profit of Paris. The change in Chad's appearance tantalizes Strether with the illusion that what he beholds – "a sharp rupture of identity," a worldly rebirth – might yield untold meanings. Chad, apparently, has been "put into a firm mould and turned successfully out" (p. 97). He looks a "young Pagan"; "a man marked out by women" (pp. 99, 98). But it is also

94

possible that he is a gentleman, for on their first meeting he is clever enough to shame Strether into seeing the uncharitable premises on which the latter's Woollett conscience operates.

While little Bilham's moral ease attracts Strether, Chad's social ease, vitality and worldly manners overwhelm him. It is as if Chad, with his singular poise and prematurely greying hair, had changed places with the older man. It is under the spell of these feelings that Strether, observing Chad in Gloriani's worldly garden in all his "calculation of effect," realizes the truth that "it was that rare youth he should have enjoyed being 'like' " (p. 133). The phrase, ironically, underscores the fact that Strether does exchange roles with Chad. For as Strether is drawn more deeply toward Madame de Vionnet, it is he who postpones their departure from Paris and Chad who announces that he is ready to leave. Ever so politely and indirectly, Chad wishes to shake off his mistress and take up his mother's challenge to return. While Strether can lose himself in the prospect of Madame de Vionnet's infinite poss-ibilities, Chad, who has got all the good he can from her, has already, mentally, put her behind him. He is properly grateful but ready to move on. For Chad, who has been "formed to please" (p. 344), lives only in the reflection of others' eyes. Thus he must nourish himself on the constant excitement of external change. By the novel's end, this descendant of Yankee buccaneers has already begun to calculate the enormous profits in the latest American "revelation" – "Advertising scientifically worked out . . . a great new force." Indeed, as an art of manipulating appearances in order to exploit by pleasing, advertising is the perfect material analogue to Chad's character. He imagines himself as the con-queror of this infinite new world – "an art like another" (p. 339). In our last glimpse of him he is tapping out a kind of sailor's jig on the street, restless to be off into the bright, amoral American future.

Taken together, Chad and Strether represent twin poles of American aspiration. It is no accident that they serve as surrogate father and son to one another, nor that they are both attracted to and empowered by the same women. Their mutual fascination and common utopian rhetoric reflect the fact that the same cul-tural forces have nurtured and supported them both. Chad's drive toward material domination and possession has its spiritual cor-relative in Strether's will to 're-see' and so mentally to repossess the world. Both, in fact, end by assimilating the plunder of Europe to higher aims. While for Chad, Madame de Vionnet is an acquisition whose person enhances his own imperious powers, for Strether she is an object who enhances his imaginative, or celebratory, ones. Although Strether acquits his moral obligation to her by admonishing Chad to stay with her, it is clear that both men are soon to be free of the burden of any personal engagement with her.

But for all this, the opposition between Chad and Strether remains in force. In fact, their similarities make all the more necessary the central contrast they embody between the promiscuity of material reality and the exclusivity of moral idealism. For all his polish, Chad is "none the less only Chad . . . of the strict human order" (p. 322). He is the advance guard of that category of Americans that James foresaw as "looming up – dim, vast, portentious – in their millions – like gathering waves – the barbarians of the Roman Empire."[30] But Chad's view of Strether continues to remind us of the special light which falls on the older man.

It is crucial to Strether's function that he should come to serve as a moral standard for others, a man whose will to "see" convinces them that he has some special power over their lives. Madame de Vionnet believes that if she keeps Strether near her Chad will stay, but more than this, she wishes to live up to his estimation of her, wishes to seem sublime in his eyes. Waymarsh seeks his blessing before he goes off with the Pococks. Chad calls him "a noble eccentric," and can only hint the truth of his own future intentions in the face of Strether's reminder of the debt the young man owes to Marie de Vionnet. In one form or another, all the characters seem to endorse Miss Gostrey's culminating response: "I can't indeed resist you" (p. 345).

Thus Strether's resistance to things as they are, while dramatized as a personal revolt, serves as moral exemplum for others within the novel's structure. By the end of the book his "choice" is seen to be the only significant one around. It is not only that he opposes the codes and values others live by, but that there are witnesses whose deference to him implicitly validates his judgment. This is quite different from the resistance of an Anna Karenina or even an Emma Bovary to things as they are; a resistance defined as only personal and ultimately self-defeating, and whose fatal consequences their authors draw out to the limit.

Given Strether's association with the moral ambition of his fore-bears, his dream of what might have been seems an attempt, both personal and supra-personal, to turn social failure into spiritual triumph.

The earlier prophetic vision that saw America as the fulfillment of a utopian dream – whether of seventeenth-century millenarian-ism or nineteenth-century democratic progress – is transmuted by James into a vision of what, in the preface to *Lady Barbarina*, he calls the "sublime consensus of the educated . . . intellectual, moral, sensual, social, political . . . There . . . in the dauntless fusions to come – is the personal drama of the future."[31] That James's idea is his own does not make it any the less representative in its conception. James's unwillingness to leave Strether in Miss Gostrey's hands only reinforces one's sense that the primary pat-tern in this story – the turn from outward dependency on public sanctions to an inner, autonomous authority – is that of the growth and development of a traditional American type of idealism in which inner conversion has what Sacvan Bercovitch has termed "representative status." In speaking of Emerson, Professor Berco-vitch has noted: "Despite his distaste for and fear of the mass of actual Americans, he did not need to dissociate himself from America because he had already dissociated the mass from the American idea."[32] Given the differences in these American ideas, I believe that an analogous strategy is at work here.

However, despite James's disclaimers, many sensitive critics have believed that Strether's final "choice" exemplifies the artistic one.[33] But surely art, as it is conceived here, is really a metaphor for the demands of the spirit, for life imagined at its most perfect pitch. In this sense all of the protagonists in this study could be artists, and have often been spoken of as reflections of the artist's predicament in America. But I believe that view approaches the problem from precisely the wrong end. In America, the artist tends to be an instance of the prophet, whose visionary impulse is associated with the nation's beginnings. As Emery Elliott has shown, long before Emerson equated the power of the seer with that of the scholar and poet, the role of man of letters was linked with the nation's sense of its special spiritual destiny. Throughout the eighteenth century the clergy and men of letters not only saw themselves in the same light, used similar techniques and verbal devices, but "were sometimes even the same people . . . the moral and spiritual role the American writers inherited became a significant characteristic of those writers and their works."[34] In 'The Prospect for Peace,' Joel Barlow "projected a future in which the poets would lead America to her destiny as the holy seat of culture and religion until Judgment Day."[35] And this "bond between religious belief and serious literature has remained strong until our time."[36] Thus whatever can be considered proto-typical of an artist's consciousness in Strether melds with visionary aspiration – but only to reinforce our sense of his stoic futility.

"To what do you go home?" Maria Gostrey asks Strether. "I don't know. There will always be something. . . . A great difference – no doubt" (p. 344). Ultimately, Strether's "great difference" returns him to another wilderness, but this time one entirely of the mind or spirit, a place in which to contemplate what is not.

Like Hester or Huck – or Ishmael – Strether ends a spiritual orphan. The impossibility of realizing his vision turns out to be precisely what fuels it. His authenticity, the shape of his consciousness, comes to depend upon keeping this tension alive.

This finale forces us to reconsider once again the cost of American moral idealism. For however delicately put, Strether's loyalty to a dream of life as it ought to be rather thatn as it is can inevitably be re-conceived as an image of isolating self-righteousness.[37]

In summarizing his sense of James's personal quest, F. R. Leavis used terms that do not seem inappropriate to Strether's own fate. "Essentially he [James] was in quest of an ideal society, an ideal civilization [where manners are] the outward notation of a spiritual and intellectual fineness." But as neither English nor American society measured up to this ideal he developed into "something like a paradoxical recluse, a recluse living socially in the midst of society."[38] For Leavis, this situation represented what he considered to be the human failure of the late works. And it is worth noting, in the complex relation that exists between author and character, that though these terms soften the outline of that self-righteous aspiration noted above, they nevertheless provide us with a poignant image of its crippling power.[39]

In the conclusion to *The Renaissance*, Pater describes the nature of the modern, individual consciousness, in terms that might at first glance be thought to define Strether's own: "The whole scope of observation is dwarfed into the narrow chambers of the individual mind. Experience, already reduced to a group of impressions, is ringed round for each one of us by that thick wall of personality through which no real voice has ever pierced on its way to us, or from us to that which we can only conjecture to be without. Every one of those impressions is the impression of the individual in his isolation, each mind keeping as a solitary prisoner its own dream of a world."[40] The pathos as well as the power of this description surely lies in Pater's sense that it is a human predicament which all (who have the capacity to "see") must share. The cost of aesthetic joy lies in its dangerous tendency toward solipsism, a darker side of the celebration of the self.

However, *The Ambassadors* moves not toward a recognition of the problems inherent in modern consciousness, but rather toward a restoration of the Emersonian claim that consciousness provides its own sanctification. If there is any triumph to be heard in Strether's last cry, "Then there we are," it is in the freedom from doubt that his vision fosters. Although Strether's dream issues in human failure, as we have seen, what he takes back to America is not a new recognition of himself and his limitations, but quite the reverse: a more absolute vision of ideal possibility and a deeper disgust with the world as it is.

Closing the Circle: *The Great Gatsby*

I think that voice held him most, with its fluctuating warmth, because it couldn't be over-dreamed – that voice was a deathless song.

"Not in time is the race progressive," Emerson proclaimed in 1839,[1] and Fitzgerald's novel might be conceived as a latter-day meditation on that persistent American faith in the power of the individual to transcend his history, to create himself anew, for which Emerson's early essays serve as master text. For despite standard interpretations, *The Great Gatsby* seems to me no simple dramatization of either the moral futility of the American dream of success, nor the destruction of innocent aspiration in a fallen world; but, in fact, the most historically self-conscious considera-tion, among all these novels, of the contradictory nature of American idealism and the social cost of its attempt to subdue the facts of history to the faith of myth.

The ideal American of Emerson's radical essays[2] is urged to transcend all temporal limitations *now*, to become his own re-deemer through an immediate act of visionary possession that obliterates time by locating man in the eternal fullness of the present moment. Like the "blade of grass or the blowing rose," man comes into his true inheritance by living "with nature in the present, above time."[3]

Emerson's conviction that the burden of time fractures con-sciousness and diminishes identity allows him to make his central denial of the power of history as a determinant in the shape of our lives. To the Emerson of the early essays, history has no delimiting force, for "being is without bounds."[4] "When a thought of Plato becomes a thought to me – when a truth that fired the soul of Pindar fires mine, time is no more."[5] Thus, in his journal he can assert, "There is no history. Only biography."[6] For "if the whole of history is in one man, it is all to be explained from individual experience."[7] Moreover, biography itself is not a circumstantial record of time, place and parental antecedents, but of the power of the individual mind to free itself from these constraints in a spiral of upward progress that assimilates lower forms of experience to higher.

Thus, "Nature," the most programmatic expression of Emerson's metaphysics, moves from man's use of the natural world, "Commodity" ("All parts incessantly work into each other's hands for the profit of man") to man's at-oneness with its power, "Spirit" ("The Supreme Being does not build up nature around us, but puts it forth through us. . . . Who can set bounds to the possibilities of man?"). In this self-generating order, mind closes the gap between itself and matter by translating the entire natural world into spiritualized will. ("Know then that the world exists for you. . . . As fast as you conform your life to the pure idea in your mind, that will unfold its great proportions.")[8]

It has often been noted that Emerson's version of the self-reliant soul, redeemed through a renewal of his capacity for vision ("The ruin or the blank that we see when we look at nature is in our own eye")[9] was a response to Franklin's prescription for autonomy through material acquisition. However, the mode of resistance Emerson develops to the commercial ethos is not dialectical but inclusive, not so much an answer to Franklin as a transposition of his ambition into spiritual, but none-the-less acquisitive, terms.[10] Emerson takes the familiar pattern of self-sufficient economic man rising by his own bootstraps to become proprietor of the world's goods and transposes it into the inner man's ascent to visionary possession of the world. ("Miller owns this field, Locke that, and Manning the woodland beyond. But none of them owns the landscape. There is a property in the horizon which no man has but he whose eye can integrate all the parts, that is, the poet.")[11] He often speaks of the soul in figures drawn from the market principles of his own day.[12] His use of mercantile metaphors to express spiritual activity should remind us that in metaphor both sides of the comparison are active; that these metaphors seek to encompass two worlds, even as they subdue one to the other. Their recurrence suggests not only how deeply Emerson was embedded in the very structures he sought to resist, but, even more importantly, I believe, how great was his need to overcome the dualism of American experience (so crass in its materialism, so stubborn in its ideals) by assimilating one to the other with all the poetic power he could command.

In like manner, Jay Gatsby, born of his Platonic conception of himself but nourished on the meretricious commodities of popular fantasy, rises in his quest for a transcendent identity from one level of experience to another. From the idolization of a dime-novel cowboy hero, he progresses to the filiopietism, and patronage, of a debauched pioneer – a millionaire speculator in precious metals. Initiated into the world and its betrayals through Dan Cody and his paramour Ella Kaye, Gatsby climbs higher, aspiring to the thing that lies behind or beyond earthly show. But Gatsby is no Ahab bursting through the world's pasteboard mask in search of the moral essence of the universe. His vision represents a kind of aestheticized materialism – the pursuit of a grail which conjoins wealth and power with all the beauty, vitality, and wonder of the world, which he incarnates in the fragile loveliness of the rich, well-born American girl.

Gatsby's biography can thus be read as an ironic recapitulation of the blueprint for spiritual ascent that Emerson lays out in 'Nature.' And just as Emerson's assimilationist ethos works to deny problems of conflict, or dualism, by obliterating all tension between inidividual will and the world's resistance (the latter is termed the "NOT-ME" and includes everything but the individual soul, i.e., "nature and art, all other men and my own body"),[13] so it does for Gatsby, the gangster-idealist, who claims for himself the power to dominate space and time, to repeat the past at will and bring the natural world (microcosmically expressed in East and West Egg) under his imaginative dominion.

It is this Emersonian myth of the individual as sovereign state, inviolable to the conditions and categories of other lives; that Fitzgerald presents as the persistent dream-wish of our national life. It is a vision of freedom that is not only cast as a backward longing but is also, paradoxically, reaffirmed precisely by that historical consciousness which must attest to its failure.

In keeping with its retrospective mode, the ending of Fitzgerald's novel reverses the equivocal pattern of its predecessors. Turning the figure inside out, as it were, it claims as the sole American reality the very dream it seeks to disown – a dream whose futility, of course, has been demonstrated in Gatsby's history. Gatsby's failure does not provide us with an opening to new experience by liberating us in any way from an ideology that no longer serves, but quite the reverse. Nick's epilogue provides us with an elegy for Gatsby – and by extension our own dreaming selves – which keeps alive the very form of that aspiration we have seen issuing in a wasteland of social and moral emptiness.

Lying on the beach in a posture that recalls his hero's last moments, Nick merges past with present as he recapitulates and comments upon Gatsby's dream. Historically sensitive, Nick can equate Gatsby's abortive attempt to recover the moment when he first incarnated his dreams in Daisy with the visionary sight of America itself; a recognition that depends upon Nick's own capacity for envisaging mythic truth. As darkness melts "the inessential houses" on the shore, he gives himself to an imaginative projection that conflates Gatsby's experience with that of the first Dutch sailors beholding the virgin green of the new land. In turn, they are universalized as "man . . . compelled into an aesthetic contemplation he neither understood nor desired . . ."[14] Nick thus enacts for us the process whereby the physical and ambiguous fact – the land itself, history's last frontier, alternately a virgin and a panderer – becomes spiritualized in the vision of the beholder.

But Nick's epiphany is just that: a moment out of time. Gatsby's mistake was in trying to domesticate it. What he could not know is that such an assimilation of sight to vision, of temporality to eternity is inevitably hopeless. Although Nick brings to these final paragraphs his historical awareness of the impossibility of such a permanent conjunction – of Daisy being anything other than what she is – his tone, suffused with yearning, draws us back toward the dream that he says already lay behind Gatsby, "somewhere back in that vast obscurity beyond the city, where the dark fields of the republic rolled on under the night" (p. 182).

Within the final paragraphs that lead to the circular paradox of the book's last line there is a shift in subject, pronoun, and tense, reinforced by a repetition of images, which conflates Gatsby's fate with ours and not only makes clear his representative status as the visionary of the America within, but insists that the central truth of our history lies in our continuing thralldom to the belief that a new world will generate a new man. The "he" of the penultimate paragraph, describing Gatsby's historical innocence ("he did not know"), becomes the all-inclusive "we" of the continuous, if contradictory present, denoting alike reader, narrator, and every character we have met in the book: "So we beat on, boats against the current, borne back ceaselessly into the past" (p. 182).[15]

Furthermore, the fatalism which underlies this imagery of recurrence, of going forward to go back, is echoed in the circular structure of the entire narrative. Exemplifying the pattern of the book's last line, Nick's chronicle moves forward through the unfolding events of the summer of 1922 only to carry us back further in time as he tries to unravel the origins of his mysterious neighbor.[16] But the final and earliest fact of Gatsby's history – Jimmy Gatz's effort at self-improvement, annotated in the Hopalong Cassidy book which his father brings to his funeral – no more explains his transformation into Jay Gatsby than does the shivering wasted figure of Henry Gatz himself. It is not from the evidence at hand, but from Nick's capacity for empathetic understanding, his visionary sympathy, that he recovers the source of Gatsby's aspiration in the original meaning of America. So the circularity of the composition completes itself by carrying us back to the book's beginning (the prologue occurs about two years after Gatsby's death) in which both Gatsby's problematic end and Nick's imaginative awe of the gorgeous possibilities he represents are established.

Alan Trachtenberg has observed that the tension between myth and history is central to all Fitzgerald's work; that myth and history project two opposing modes of consciousness, two ways of knowing the world which provide perspectives on each other.[17] Although I do not believe Fitzgerald to have been as disinterested an observer of American life as this definition implies, it seems an especially suggestive insight for understanding how the interplay of the novel, despite our contrary expectations, prepares us for an ending in which history comes to validate myth, and myth to ennoble history. For though the major distinction between myth and history would seem to be dramatized in the neighborly opposition of Gatsby, the man of mythic action – whose home, with Gothic library, Norman towers, Marie Antoinette music room "is a world complete in itself"[18] – and Nick Carraway, the ironic historian of reserved judgments and limited hopes – whose utilitarian bungalow houses the secrets of Midas and Morgan in the form of brokerage reports – their characters interpenetrate one another like the cut and uncut grass of their adjacent lawns.

If Gatsby is god-like, with his sun chariot car, his pink and gold accoutrements, his Olympian feasts,[19] he is also a gilded Jimmy Gatz, self-created through getting. The corrupt materialism that dogs his aspirations creates morally antithetical meanings for all the symbols that surround him – gold, most obviously, representing both the impersonal energy and glory of the sun and a base metal dug out of the earth which has the most ancient associations with carnal power and avarice. For Gatsby is, finally, neither the hero of an Emersonian essay nor a fabulous Jamesian force like Maggie Verver, whose consciousness is so absolute that it ends by subduing (or strangling) the entire natural world within its embrace. Rather, he is himself the historically determined image of such a figure, trapped by circumstances that mock the gorgeous possibilities of his dreams, and are themselves conceptualized by Nick, the historian, as nightmare myth – a spreading hell of dust and ashes which devours the spirit as it does the body and turns living men into impoverished specters, indistinguishable from the industrial wasteland they inhabit. Indeed, the very form that Gatsby's mythic impulse takes, his aspiration to evade the present by repeating the past, reflects the popular taste on which he has been nourished. For, as Richard Hofstadter has noted, this longing was historically conditioned, bred out of post-Civil War disillusion with the corruption of the Gilded Age and had been part of American sentimental and popular rhetoric at least since Bryan.[20]

But what seems generally to have been overlooked among critics' observations provides, to my mind, the most significant historical perspective on Gatsby's character. This is not the obvious fact of his crypto-gangster dealings, but the implications to be drawn from the social form which his enterprise takes. The constant irruption of the telephone into Gatsby's public life reminds us that despite his apparent isolation, Gatsby does not act alone. The calls that link him to agents in the West hint at a labyrinth of "gonnections" which replicates in negative the interlocking corporate structures of the legitimate world in which Nick labors at his more conventional version of the bond business. It is these "gonnections" that provide the pedestal of wealth on which Gatsby seems to stand in lonely splendor. From this perspective his heroic individualism is a self-deluding sham, fittingly expressed in the meretricious guise of "castle," car, and clothing. It represents a popular dream-wish which serves as a defense against the dislocations and complexities of a changing society.

As the common middle-class ideal of the self-made man rising through his own efforts to a position of social and economic power (whose prototype we saw in Robin Molineux) was becoming an obsolete reality, so his fictional counterpart was more intensely romanticized in the image of the lone cowboy or outlaw, loyal to his own moral code and enduring a solitary existence in the wilderness. In *The Incorporation of America*, Alan Trachtenberg has shown how this popular myth persisted to deny the reality of corporate control which arrived with post-Civil War industrial expansion.[21]

Gatsby, through his two surrogate fathers, the buccaneer Dan Cody and the gangster Meyer Wolfsheim, unites the imagery of free-wheeling plunder in the Gilded Age to that of the Jazz Age, but by traditional codes of loyalty, both these fathers ultimately betray him. Dan Cody promises him a legacy, but the debauched old frontiersman no longer has the mind or will to ensure its disposition. Wolfsheim, who claims to have "made" Gatsby, to look on him as a son, will not risk appearing at his funeral. Far from personifying those qualities of rugged individualism associated with the frontier myth, both Cody and Wolfsheim are victims of "forces" and "circumstances" which they seem unwilling or unable to control. When Gatsby met Cody the latter was already a vacuous, played-out figure, captive to a scheming woman, Ella Kaye – whose name, it has often been noted, rhymes with Daisy Fay. Meyer Wolfsheim's name, like his molar cufflinks, may allude to the ferocity of the forest, but he is more akin to the ambiguous 'grandma' of the 'Little Red Riding Hood' fairy tale than to a feral beast. In his office, he hides from Nick behind a woman and then excuses himself from attending Gatsby's funeral with a string of sentimental platitudes worthy of Uriah Heep.

Ultimately, Gatsby's relation to these fathers seems more contractual than personal. Their betrayals are largely failures of obligation; on either side, there is little energy of personal feeling. As Nick learns when he confronts Wolfsheim, questions of affection and emotional concern only mask the real interest – which is business. ("I raised him up out of nothing, right out of the gutter," says Wolfsheim proudly. "I saw right away he was a fine-appearing, gentlemanly young man, and when he told me he was an Oggsford I knew I could use him good" [p. 172].) Gatsby's relations with these men, as with his agents, turn out to be a paradigm of the larger social order depicted in the book – a collection of isolated beings whose interconnections are coded in terms of the use each can make of the other.

Yet, if the Great Gatsby, viewed from an historical perspective, is only a self-deluded con-man, the energy of his delusion matches the mythic scale of America's own. Guilt-free but deeply secretive, guileless but amorally corrupt, Gatsby embodies the essential contradictions of our national history and our national faith.

The fact that Fitzgerald foregrounds Gatsby's divided nature makes all the more acute, at this historical juncture, the moral ambiguity at the heart of the Emersonian myth of the visionary self – a myth for which the ever-expanding natural wealth of the country serves, within the book as it does within our history, as seductive validation.[22] In Gatsby we can see that the structure of incorporation, upon which Emersonian transcendence depends, ignores dualism and denies conflict at its (and our) peril. To disengage from the particulars of the social struggle, is not only to leave the field to the energies of the most rapacious and cunning; it is also to dismiss the significance of that traditional civilized enterprise which concerns itself with modestly enlarging the sphere of moral nuance and moral valuation, against which all action must ultimately be measured. Thus Gatsby has no qualms in putting his criminal career at the service of his faithful pursuit of "the promises of life." This is not merely a question of ends justifying means. The means for Gatsby need no justification – they may be socially awkward, but morally they do not count. Like the other forms of dissociation we have noted, Gatsby's protects him from any need for self-confrontation, and so keeps his dream alive.

His unblinking indifference to the ugly and criminal aspects of his own nature serves as the psychic counterpart to America's historical innocence about the sources of its own wealth, its tie to the exploitative realities of a fallen world, which Daisy (the driver of the "death car") comes to embody. Like his country's, Gatsby's illusions about the self and its powers are matched by his illusions about history, by his faith that "of course you can" repeat the past (p. 111). He may be better than the other characters ("worth the whole damn bunch put together" [p. 154]), but Nick's obsessive ambivalence toward him ("I disapproved of him from beginning to end") would seem to suggest that ultimately he is not good enough.

That Gatsby is not just the mythic embodiment of an American type but personifies the outline of our national consciousness is demonstrated by his structural relation to the other characters and, in particular, to the narrator, Nick Carraway.

Despite differences of class and taste, despite their apparent mutually antagonistic purposes, all the characters in this book are defined by their nostalgia for and sense of betrayal by some lost, if only dimly apprehended promise in their past – a sense of life's possibilities toward which only Gatsby has retained the ingenuous faith and energy of the true seeker. It is in the difference between vision and sight, between the longing for self-transcendence and the lust for immediate gain – for sexual, financial, or social domination – that Nick, his chronicler and witness, finds the moral distinction which separates Gatsby from the "foul dust" of the others who float in his wake. And this moral dichotomy runs through the structure of the entire work. For the rapacious nature of each of the others, whether crude, desperate, arrogant or false, is finally shown to be a function of their common loss of vision, their blurred or displaced sense of possibilities – punningly symbolized in the enormous empty retinas of the occulist-wag, Dr T. J. Eckleburg. Thus Gatsby and those who eddy around him are, reciprocally, positive and negative images of one another; but whether faithless or true all are doomed by the wasteful, self-deluding nature of the longing which controls their lives and which when it fails leaves its adherents utterly naked and alone, "contiguous to nothing."

However, Nick's insight into the distinction between Gatsby and others does not free him from his own involvement in the world he observes. His acute awareness of his own self-division (toward Gatsby as toward all the others) turns out to be the mirror inversion of his subject's unconscious one; it accounts for the sympathetic bond between them. And just as Gatsby's ingenuous self-dissociation is the ground of his faith that the moral complexity of the world can be subdued to his imaginative vision (Daisy's feelings for Tom are only a case of the "personal"), so Nick's self-division leads him to ultimately reject the world ("I wanted no more . . . privileged glimpses into the human heart"). They are twin poles of All or Nothing – Gatsby's hope is Nick's despair.

Nick's kinship to Gatsby is established in the prologue, where his own version of "infinite hope" – the capacity to reserve judgment – is implicitly contrasted with Gatsby's "extraordinary gift for hope." This latter is not, says Nick, in a self-deprecating reference, a matter of any "flabby impressionability," but of a romantic readiness such as he has never found in any other person "and which it is not likely I shall ever find again" (p. 2). The phrase tells us that Nick too is a seeker, that the strength of Gatsby's romantic energy resonates against Nick's own muted but responsive sensibility. Indeed, Nick's most immediately distinguishing trait, his consciousness of the flux of time as a series of intense, irrecoverable moments, is keyed to a romantic pessimism whose melancholy note is struck on his thirtieth birthday, when he envisions his future as a burden of diminishing returns leading inexorably to loneliness, enervation, and death.[23]

Moreover, it is Nick's own confused responsiveness to his cousin's sexual power and charm that allows him subsequently to understand Gatsby's equation of Daisy with all that is most desirable under the heavens – ultimately with the siren song of the American continent. Nick cannot help but be compelled by the buoyant vitality which surrounds her and the glowing sound of her "low, thrilling voice," which sings with "a promise that she had done gay, exciting things just a while since and that there were gay exciting things hovering in the next hour" (p. 10). But, as the shadow of his double, Nick's response to Daisy is qualified by his discomforting awareness of the illusory and deceptive in her beauty. Her smirking insincerity, her banal chatter, the alluring whiteness of her expensive clothes – most of all, the languid boredom which enfolds her life – suggest a willing captivity, a lazy self-submission to a greater power than her own magical charms: the extraordinary wealth and physical arrogance that enable Tom Buchanan to dominate her. And Nick's visceral dislike for the man Daisy has given herself to, fanned by his intellectual and moral scorn for Tom's crude attempt to master "ideas" as he does horses and women, allies him with, as it prefigures, Gatsby's bland disregard of Tom as a factor in Daisy's existence.

Nick's experience of Daisy is, in fact, commensurate with his experience of the East. For like Daisy and her husband, transplanted Westerners who have drifted to the new center of energy and power, the East turns out to be the America of the moment – America experienced as a wilderness of opportunity, with all the ambiguity this implies.

West Egg, with its raw wealth and promiscuous mix of classes and types, is a metaphoric reminder of frontier society; while East

Egg has all the decorum and snobbery of those who have "arrived" at least one generation earlier. (The Buchanans live in a house built by "Demaine, the oil man.") Together, the Eggs, with their smashed bottoms, serve as a metaphor for American actuality – the social barnyard of the present in which money and power breed ever-more-corrupt versions of a once-bright historical 'ideal. . . But from a distance their shore lines are enticing.

Nick comes East for the same reason that his forebears went West – he is restless, seeking adventure, excitement, freedom from the monotonous regularity and control of an established pattern of life and established social expectations. In the East he feels like a path-finder. There is a sense of things growing faster, of time and motion speeded up (as in a movie), of unexpected if illusory joy. The towers of New York rise "up across the river in white heaps and sugar lumps . . . The city seen from the Queensboro Bridge is always the city seen for the first time, in its first wild promise of all the mystery and beauty in the world" (p. 69). Like the aura that emanates from Daisy, it is a magical place where anything can happen. "Even Gatsby could happen" (p. 69). And yet the ugliness, greed, and human sterility he discovers in this raucous wilderness are far worse than anything in the grey world of worn-out traditions that he has left behind.

Nick's response to the moral ambiguity which surrounds him is to stress his own self-division. At the party in Myrtle Wilson's apartment, he feels himself to be both "within and without, simultaneously enchanted and repelled by the inexhaustible variety of life." But this static tension of opposite impulses is rather a resistance to than an acceptance of the blurring of distinctions, the vulgarities in taste and manners that constitute the scene before him.

It is characteristic that the only action Nick records of himself during this long evening, in which Tom manages to break Myrtle's nose, is to wipe away a speck of shaving lather from Mr Mckee's cheek – a tiny impulse which has been gathering force in him all evening long. In its obsession with categories of social order (shaving cream belongs in the bathroom not the living-room, alludes to a private not a public act), it epitomizes Nick's intense self-control as well as his profound revulsion from the social squalor he perceives in "the inexhaustible variety of life."[24]

Nick's discomfort with the actual, his preference for imaginary

encounters with romantic women to a real affair with a girl in his
office (terminated at the first whiff of unpleasant consequences),
suggests both the threat which any morally complex situation holds
for him and the messy, disappointing vulgarity in which reality is
always served up to him.[25]

Gatsby thus provides Nick with a grand alter-ego. Plunging into
the world's "vast, vulgar, and meretricious beauty," he recreates
it through a domineering faith in his own vision of its meaning.
Nick, for whom perception replaces action, comes to see what
Gatsby sees, but can only imitate the passion of his hero's sacrifice
through his own chaste withdrawal.[26]

Although some critics claim to find in Nick's return to the
Midwest a saving alternative to the futility of Gatsby's example,
this reading seems to me to be itself a wishful dream out of a more
sober historical moment. For the Midwest of Nick's allusions is
hardly the moral alternative to the East that it has often been
taken to be.[27] Rather, the moral distinction at issue in this novel,
as in the others discussed, turns out to be a choice between the
world or one's vision of it – not between what life might offer in
one or another geographical context.

The actual West, we are told at the beginning of the book, is a
place of chronic anxiety, the "ragged edge of the universe," where
an evening is hurried "toward its close, in a continually disappointed anticipation or else in sheer nervous dread of the
moment itself" (p. 13). Daisy and Jordan, with their cool, impersonal "absence of desire," buoyed by privilege and wealth, serve as
the vanguard of a process symbolized in the drift from West to
East that includes all characters in the book. More than malaise,
it is a creeping spiritual paralysis that shows itself in chronic
anxiety and dread before it reaches the acute stage of anomie that
Nick finds at the pinnacle of American social power. Ironically, it
is the restless rich, with their greater freedom to experience life's
possibilities, to seek fulfillment in action and experimentation, who
most clearly reveal the aridity at the heart of the American faith
that the way to wealth is the way to a new status, a new essence,
that through wealth one may rise "to a loftier place in the mysterious hierarchy of human worth."[28] They have moved farther and
faster from the old America that Nick recognizes in the dreams of
Gatsby and the still unquenched longings of the Wilsons – the
coarse vitality of Myrtle's body, the "damp gleam of hope" in

George's eyes. It is, therefore, metaphorically fitting that it should be Daisy and Tom who together cause the "holocaust" in which these three give up their lives.

Nick reminds us at the end of the book that all the characters are Westerners, "that this has been a story of the West, after all" (p. 177). I take this to mean a story of the decline and fall of American hopes – the West in its largest sense standing for the westward course of empire, for the dream of America as mankind's last best hope for social and moral redemption.[29] Nick's retreat to the West thus repeats the pattern of continued attachment to a hopeless ideal implicit in Gatsby's "sacrificial" death.

For only in the glow of Nick's memory does his old home become that exhilarating landscape whose "sharp wild brace" had once thrilled him with a commensurate sense of his own being. Just as Nick's modesty is reminiscent of Strether's, so his retreat to a lost world that exists only in the privacy of his imagination is, as it was for Strether, a reconfirmation of his youthful identity (the mingling of sensation and vision, the moral simplifications of his father) and a rejection of the imperfect, messy and ambiguous tangle of adult life.[30]

Although ambiguity is not the keynote of Nick's sensibility, as a first-person narrator he evokes its presence by stressing metaphoric equivalents for its effects: the blurred and drunken comings and goings at the Washington Heights apartment; the dazzling confusion of names and faces at Gatsby's parties; and, finally, his own exhausted sympathy following the climactic confrontation between Gatsby and the Buchanans at the Hotel Plaza.

As Tom tries to unmask his rival by reducing him to "Mr Nobody from Nowhere" and Gatsby seeks to establish the priority of his claim to Tom's wife, one feels, for the first and only time in the book, a genuine dramatic tension in the triangular interplay of the characters. The moment that Tom brings Gatsby to earth, so to speak, by gloating over his shoddy underworld life is the moment when Gatsby, suddenly vulnerable, seems most humanly alive, fending off Tom's attacks while reaching out for Daisy's love. Concomitantly, Daisy becomes interestingly pathetic in the first authentic response we have from her as she admits to having loved Tom while loving Gatsby too. But Gatsby cannot recognize the truth of what Daisy says, cannot see as Nick does that she never intended leaving Tom for him, "never intended doing anything at all." It is this final note of stubborn resistance to the fact that his vision cannot shape the subsequent flow of Daisy's life, that there is an irreducible gap between the world and his will, which, paradoxically, seals Nick's allegiance to him and, with Tom laughing in the background, tips the scene toward moral melodrama. The incipient ambiguity crystallizes into a chivalric combat between Tom, the black knight of the world, and Gatsby, the silver knight of the spirit, fighting for the hand of the virgin princess who can empower the ruler of the land.[31]

By making Tom – so brutal and duplicitous himself – the grand inquisitor of Gatsby's character, Fitzgerald effectively draws our sympathy toward Gatsby's idealism and sidesteps the deeper moral issues at stake in this confrontation. For at its core Gatsby's imperial fantasy is more profoundly and grandly amoral than Tom Buchanan has the capacity to imagine. Its claims are radical, based on an absolute disregard for the consequences of one's actions; on a faith that motives alone matter; and that these are to be tested only by the conviction of one's own perception of truth. Gatsby's character presents us with a debased, modern-dress version of the old antinomian question that so troubled Hawthorne. The community may be wrong, uncharitable, or as corrupt as it is here shown to be – its power and authority vested in a class personified by the domineering arrogance and intellectual cretinism of Tom Buchanan; but the antinomian figure who opposes it is also inevitably a part of it and bears its marks. Gatsby's criminal nature links him to the self-corruption of Tom, Jordan, and Daisy – representatives of the world he longs to conquer. (Among the many parallels between Gatsby and the Buchanans, the most striking is that all three are killers. As Gatsby is said to have been responsible for killing someone, so, by the end of the story, are both Daisy and Tom.)

His indifference to their true nature – at the least, his failure to perceive what Daisy's bond to her husband indicates about her – is crucially linked to his denial of his own reprobate actions. For any self-recognition on Gatsby's part would inevitably lead to an acknowledgment of his community with others. To come to terms with one's own moral nature is, as Hawthorne put it in another context, to open an intercourse with the world, while to evade oneself in the name of a higher truth or a brighter perception is to evade the world's intrinsic presence, the irreducible otherness to which one is nevertheless bound. The denial of such human connection truly creates a Valley of Ashes, where even the small graces of a Michaelis or an Owl-eyes will no longer be found.

It is really not enough to say, as so many critics have with Nick, that Gatsby's ingenuous faith redeems his criminal nature, or that his is merely the immorality of the law, not the heart.[32] As the orthodox Puritan community recognized, both inner spirit and outward decency are necessary for the establishment of human community.[33] To sanctify Gatsby's divided nature in this manner is to give oneself to the same kind of self-delusion he does – and in so doing to ignore those very complexities that raise the book far above the level of naive culture myth. For it is Gatsby's divided nature that sets him apart from the Buchanans. They have no ingenuous aspirations. But Fitzgerald goes out of his way to let us know that Gatsby's criminality is not the passing expedient he himself takes it for; that it is as much a part of his life and nature as is his idealism. Nor, unlike Hester Prynne's adultery, does his bootlegging oppose one moral standard to another; in his case, an ancient, habitual social practice challenging an impossibly utopian and unenforceable law. Gatsby is a businessman (hence the comic irony in Wolfsheim's celebration of his "Oggsford" appearance; it makes a respectable front) whose business is crime – and this means whatever illegal enterprise comes to hand. Today he would be dealing in narcotics and selling arms to terrorists.

Nothing so clearly delineates the quality of Gatsby's amorally dissociated nature as his reaction to Myrtle Wilson's death. Nick notes with surprise, and at first with disgust, that Gatsby shows no concern for the woman who was killed by Daisy's reckless driving. "He spoke as if Daisy's reaction was the only thing that mattered" (p. 144). However, once it is clear that Daisy was driving, that Gatsby did not actually run over the woman, Nick's condemnation also fades. Yet who drove the car is surely not the only subject of concern here. It is Gatsby's unwavering focus on Daisy, and his concomitant lack of feeling for the dead woman, that is so chilling. Moreover, what is both heroic and outrageous in his plan to assume the blame for Daisy's driving is his utter disregard, not merely of the consequences to himself (should his car be identified) but of common standards of truth, justice, and personal responsibility. In his attempt to absolve Daisy of guilt, Gatsby arrogates to himself the communal power of judge and jury. As if he were indeed a god, he asserts the supremacy of his own behavioral standard over all others. His action is the idealistic twin to his darker, but equally amoral underworld pragmatism which conceives Meyer Wolfsheim – the man who played, in Nick's ingenuous phrase, "with the faith of fifty million people" by fixing the World Series of 1919 – as a smart man who "just saw the opportunity."

Gatsby's indifference to the fate of the woman bleeding in the road or to those who might be mourning for her, is part of his larger indifference to the reality of the entire material world – including, as we have noted, to his own physical being. And it seems to be the very grandeur of this disdain for Emerson's "NOT-ME" that elicits Nick's subsequent judgment that Gatsby is "worth the whole damn bunch put together." It is surely out of loyalty to Gatsby's private code that Nick himself remains silent at the inquest, concealing Gatsby's connection to Daisy (and Myrtle's to Tom) as he does the truth about who was driving; just as he later refrains from confronting Tom with the truth of Daisy's guilt for Myrtle's death.

With Nick as Gatsby's loyal partisan, Fitzgerald, in effect, has it both ways. He gives us enough evidence to see through Gatsby, to make us aware of his terrible failings, but he cannot quite free himself, as he cannot free Nick, from the power of Gatsby's attraction. For Nick to speak out at the inquest would be to destroy not only Daisy (his social kin) but also his own identification with Gatsby, and thus an aspect of himself, by reducing Gatsby's relations with Daisy to the vulgar level of a West Egg gossip item. The issue here, it seems to me, is not Fitzgerald's over-identification with the romance of money or the glamour of the twenties, as some have charged, but that of the power of a cultural myth to which Gatsby's very anomalies enthrall us. For despite Nick's scrupulous reminders that he disapproved of Gatsby from beginning to end, Gatsby's death – a pointless and absurd sacrifice – is described in terms of the passing of a nature god, or a pastoral hero. The mythic motifs that surround his end, from the climactic confrontation scene to the shooting in the swimming pool and the funeral itself, are reminders of the revolution of the seasons (another motif of recurrence, which echoes the circular structure we have already noted), with death inevitably presaging rebirth.

Gatsby's loss of Daisy occurs on the hottest day of summer. It is a day so broiling it feels as if the earth were about to fall into the sun, or perhaps "it's just the opposite – the sun's getting colder every year" (p. 118), Tom reports, muddling the symbols but reliably predicting both Gatsby's and Daisy's fall. (Daisy's name suggests the duality of her role: its substance refers to a fragile but common field flower, its sound, 'Day's eye,' contains a metaphor for the sun.) In contrast to this climactic event, the day that follows, the day of Gatsby's death, is cool. The summer is felt to be over. There is already "an autumn flavor in the air." The rain which accompanies the funeral has generally been read as a sign of spiritual gloom and emptiness. Yet rain is also an ancient sign of fecundity and rebirth – an echo of which is heard in the anonymous funeral benediction, "Blessed are the dead that the rain falls on" (p. 176).

But it is Nick's poetic evocation of Gatsby's passing which ultimately weaves the antitheses of his life into a mythic whole, completing in imagination the assimilation of fact to spirit that Gatsby himself failed to attain in life.

There was a faint, barely perceptive movement of the water as the fresh flow from one end urged its way toward the drain at the other. With little ripples that were hardly the shadow of waves, the laden mattress moved irregularly down the pool. A small gust of wind that scarcely corrugated the surface was enough to disturb its accidental course with its accidental burden. The touch of a cluster of leaves revolved it slowly, tracing like the leg of transit, a thin red circle in the water.   (p. 163)

This is not the death of a gangster caught off-guard on an air mattress, as Tom Buchanan or the newspapers would report it. We never, in fact, see Gatsby's body in its bathing trunks; we know nothing about where the bullet got him, or the expression on his face. The paragraph is concerned only with motion – the gentlest of attending breezes wafts the "laden" mattress on its "transit" toward the drain. The language, as Robert Long has noted, is reminiscent of pastoral elegy.[34] The cluster of leaves that accompanies the movement is a harbinger of the rainy days to follow – the seasonal analogue to the hero's death, when "everything starts all over again," as Jordan Baker crisply observes. The circular motif is reiterated in the final sentence in which the mattress is "revolved by the leaves" as life by the seasons, while its trail is marked by a "thin red circle," sign and symbol of the hero's passion.

But for all the energy of his desire, Gatsby, envisaged by Nick, ends as a passive figure. He goes to the swimming pool almost as if he expected to meet his death, as if he "no longer cared." Nick's commentary makes Gatsby's career such an inevitable one, assimilating it to age-old cosmic patterns (as he later assimilates it to those of American history) that Gatsby himself is absolved of any responsibility for its course and consequences. In the end he becomes as mythically impersonal a figure as even he might have wished.

It is therefore Nick's own character that is the crucial factor in our evaluation of Gatsby's significance. For if Nick is not a credible moral guide, if his ambivalence deserves neither the reader's sympathy nor respect, then not only his attitude toward Gatsby but all the judgments he makes can be called into question. To pursue this line of reasoning to its end would be to unravel the entire fabric of the novel. With Nick no longer the mediator of our sympathy but the object of our scorn, the sense of loss he feels at the end would not be worth our time and attention. This sort of deconstruction, in which the novel devours itself, may flatter contemporary critical sensibilities, but it hardly seems to square with Fitzgerald's.[35]

However, to deny that Nick is a knave or a fool is not to accept the alternative convention that he is simply a transparent narrator who journeys from innocence to wisdom in the course of the story.[36] For no more than Gatsby's does Nick's moral education lead to any significant self-recognition or understanding, nor any concomitant gain in human sympathy. It is precisely his identification with Gatsby that prevents Nick from achieving a place in that middle ground of modest social and personal affirmation in which some critics have been eager to place him, but which, I believe, Fitzgerald withholds.

For in no other book discussed here is the novelistic world as turned in on itself as this one. Nick's retrospection effectively seals all exits. Gatsby's life is presented to us by a man for whom social actuality is a foul hell of dispirited souls and visionary possibility an inevitable delusion. Indeed, for Nick there is no human warmth but in illusion – without it life is repellent. So he imagines it for Gatsby in his moment of truth, awaiting the phone call from Daisy that "was never to arrive" and shivering "as he found what a grotesque thing a rose is and how raw the sunlight was upon the scarce created grass" (p. 162). As Wayne Booth has noted about the novel, "As it stands it can be described as either Nick's experience of Gatsby or as Gatsby's life seen by Nick. The seamless web of observation and experience creates a unity which we accept."[37] Because he is a first-person narrator, Nick's view of the world shapes and controls all other views within the text. Ultimately, his ambivalence, his reticence, his self-contradictions do not undermine the value of his response but are the very substance of it.

In regard to the centrality of Nick's role, the formulations of his consciousness, there is a comparison to be made with Marlow, the narrator of Joseph Conrad's *Heart of Darkness*. Like Nick, Marlow crosses the boundary of his conventionally ordered life to enter the precincts of another's extraordinary mental universe. It is known that Fitzgerald considered Conrad to be the major influence on the new style he had developed for *The Great Gatsby*, and that he was particularly interested in Conrad's technique for controlling and developing the narrator's point of view.[38] Yet the technical skill he absorbed from Conrad is utilized by Fitzgerald for very different ends. Fitzgerald's work, however much it benefits from the discipline of modernist literary consciousness, diverges sharply from Conrad's in the way it ultimately comes to terms with the imperatives of individual identity. Once again, in this comparison we can see a major cultural distinction between a European and an American delineation of moral options.

Marlow tells us in the course of his narrative that work is valuable because it leads to a chance to find yourself, "your own reality . . . for yourself, not for others. What no man can ever know. They can only see the mere show, and never can tell what it really means."[39] It is this subjective nature of human experience and the pathos of our inability ever to completely communicate or share it that I take to be the "haze," the larger meaning that surrounds the "glow" of the story of Kurtz.[40]

Long before he meets the fabulous ivory hunter who has gone farther into the interior than any man yet, Marlow's imagination of Kurtz takes the form of a voice. For Kurtz is known as a gifted creature, "and that of all his gifts the one that stood out preeminently, that carried with it a sense of real presence, was his ability to talk, his words – the gift of expression" (p. 113). Indeed, it is as a voice that Kurtz comes to affect Marlow, his dying discourse culminating in a cry ("The horror! The horror!") which

Marlow believes represents "the appalling face of a glimpsed truth." It conveys Kurtz's knowledge of himself and seems to reclaim his humanity on the brink of eternal darkness (p. 151). But the reality of Kurtz – this man whose ambition for change, conquest, trade, massacre, blessings, led him on to an extremity of self-exploitation that mirrors in both its depravity and its exalted ambition the nightmare adventure of European imperialism – cannot be truly comprehended by Marlow. All he can do is to suggest something of the powerful effect this extraordinary creature has had on him through the compulsion of his own narrative voice. For, says Marlow, "I have a voice, too, and for good or evil mine is the speech that cannot be silenced" (p. 97).

It is Marlow's equation of "voice" with the search for authenticity of self, the struggle to convey a sense of the complexity of being, that makes his notion of individualism the very opposite of Nick Carraway's. Whereas Marlow's hesitations and self-doubts testify to his acceptance of what is essentially ineffable in human experience, Nick's are the pretext for his scorn and disgust at human moral failure. *Heart of Darkness* ends with Marlow having salvaged something out of the abominations he has witnessed. The gain for him is a horrifying moment of self-recognition through his encounter with Kurtz – and, I would add, to the degree that his listeners understand him, the enlargement of that tissue of consciousness which, it is hoped, can sustain civilized community. For the discourse of Conrad's novella is structured as a series of interpenetrating voices momentarily emerging from the profound darkness (both internal and external) of the scene. Just as Kurtz talks on and on to Marlow, seeking to communicate something of the significance of his life, the value of Marlow's experience ultimately lies in his attempt to speak of it to the others. It is this fragile chain of discourse, voice upon voice, trying to weave the reality of the individual self into the great and terrible fabric of civilization, that represents for Marlow the authentic human task, the only real barrier to the bleak savagery at the heart of the human condition.

Thus Marlow tells his story to a communtiy of fellows, men who represent the authority of Anglo-Saxon values and traditions, yet respect him for the very inconclusiveness and strangeness of what he relates. His narrative evokes the shadow of their common darkness, and with it their need for mutual acknowledgment in the struggle for meaning each must make alone. It is this individual, essentially Sisyphean, task that represents the heroism of the middle ground and which leaves us with a sense of Marlow's accomplishment.

But Nick has neither Marlow's sense of existence as a lonely private moral struggle, nor that sentiment of community which may offer the solace of a common code of values derived from a shared past. Nick's three-generation Midwestern town is a place of apparent stability, where names are remembered and houses are identified with families. But these are only outward signs. In themselves they express neither the substance of human feeling nor the value of authentic connection. It is far more revealing of Nick's condition that his only personal tie to the Midwest is based on a misunderstanding with a girl about an engagement he never intended, and whose continued irresolution serves as pretext for his restrained relations with the morally dubious Jordan Baker. For in Nick's cautious, self-sufficient code, moral decency equates with emotional economy, honesty with self-protective discretion, freedom with isolation. And just as he epitomizes his autobiography in a few phrases about the genealogy of his family and his father's moral precepts, so he is essentially a character defined not by the moral depth of his self-awareness, as Marlow is, but by the typicality of his ethical contradictions.

Although Nick introduces himself to us as the inheritor of a tradition of genteel tolerance, the "advantages" of which his father reminds him are soon revealed to be based on the mercantile prescience of an ancestor who bought his way out of serving in the Civil War and went on to establish a successful hardware business. As much as Gatsby, and very much like the prototypical Franklin persona of *The Autobiography*, Nick is representative of the moral incongruities of our American condition. If Gatsby is the ideal national self, Nick is the more pragmatic social self – two sides of the same coin of American consciousness.

Moreover, Conrad's *Heart of Darkness* dramatizes individual identity as a dynamic process of self-encounter in which meaning is never stable nor experience predictable. Kurtz's ambitions alter as he enacts them; his savagery grows with his freedom from restraint. The solitude and silence of the jungle, the worship of the African tribe, reveal an appalling lust for adulation which he experiences as a divine and terrible addiction ("Exterminate the brutes" [p. 118]).

In contrast, Gatsby remains indifferent to the impact of others upon him. His identity is predicated on a dream which, in its grandest form, existed prior to his meeting with Daisy. Once having kissed her and "forever wed his unutterable visions to her perishable breath, his mind would never romp again like the mind of God" (p. 112). As his dream represents a faith prior to experience, so his inner life neither changes nor develops with circumstance, but seems merely to unfold in a pre-ordained pattern of success and betrayal which goes far to explain the sense of passivity and repetition that we have noted as central to the book.

Nor is Nick's identity formed out of the ambiguities and uncertainties inherent in personal struggle. While the reader may be aware that Nick's allegiance to Gatsby represents the repressed side of himself, this insight is not shared by Nick. He accounts for his loyalty only in terms of moral scruples – his judgment of Gatsby measured against the world. For true self-knowledge he substitutes a familiar kind of moral accounting. His eyes are turned outward, and personal understanding is no more his goal than it is his hero's.

In the prologue, Nick claims that he is "inclined to reserve all judgments." Yet, having said this, he thereupon makes the most inclusive judgment possible. Separating Gatsby's essence, so to speak, from the moral contamination of all the others in the book (what "preyed on Gatsby"), he prepares us for the world we are to experience by pre-defining its categories. Thus the reader's own inclination to suspend judgment in favor of sympathetic understanding is (except in the case of Gatsby) sharply curtailed. Whereas the musing, brooding style of Marlow's discourse reflects his view of existence as a fluid, morally unfathomable process that embraces all men, the near-Manichean oppositions of Nick's narrative establish a world conceived very differently. This pattern, with its emphasis on lacks and losses, its sense of deterioration from bright beginnings, cannot be understood, I believe, without reference to those peculiar American cultural conditions that encourage us to conflate individual with national experience in an image of identity which exalts aspiration as a kind of American birthright while confounding limitation with deprivation and decline.

Alan Trachtenberg has observed that America of all modern states seems to fulfill the hope of Enlightenment thinkers (Rousseau and Jefferson) that "the private person might view his own private interests for the first time in history as identical with those of the whole society." And this identity of interest provided "hope of Utopia within the American polity."[41] It is of the failure of this utopian hope to sustain itself within the American polity that drives each of the protagonists we have discussed to preserve his or her vision by projecting it onto an alternative landscape.

Conversely, it is hard to find anywhere in our classic American literature as unequivocal a recognition of the value of the every-day struggle, of the middle ground of impure but common life, as this which Marlow makes in trying to imagine Kurtz's experience of release from European society.

. . . no warning voice of a kind neighbour can be heard whispering of public opinion? These little things make all the great difference. When they are gone you must fall back upon your own innate strength, upon your own capacity for faithfulness. Of course you may be too much of a fool to go wrong – too dull even to know you are being assaulted by the powers of darkness . . . Or you may be such a thunderingly exalted creature as to be altogether deaf and blind to anything but heavenly sights and sounds. Then the earth for you is only a standing place – and whether to be like this is your loss or your gain I won't pretend to say. But most of us are neither the one nor the other. The earth for us is a place to live in, where we must put up with sights, with sounds, with smells, too, by Jove! – breathe deep hippo, so to speak, and not be contaminated. And there, don't you see? your strength comes in, the faith in your ability for the digging of unostentatious holes to bury the stuff in – your power of devotion, not to yourself, but to an obscure, back-breaking business. And that's enough. (p. 117)

"The digging of unostentatious holes" – this is what we might expect from Nick, save that Nick keeps reminding us, not of the value of the task but of the bitter negations of spirit which make it so bleak and hopeless an effort. When he speaks for duty and responsibility to others, as he does most clearly in trying to give Gatsby a decent funeral, it is to remind us of the fundamentals to which he stoically holds in the absence of even the sentiment of community among those he terms "foul dust." This image, with its connotation of disgusting, listless drift, epitomizes the quality of Nick's judgmental scorn for the human society of which he is inevitably a part.

For in this novel community as an informing social ideal exists only by negation. The outline of its absence shows most clearly in

those grand and perverse forms of social ritual which Gatsby in-
genuously convokes in his attempt to draw Daisy back to him.

As images of plenitude gone awry, Gatsby's parties afford us a
spectacle of the dream of the American garden collapsing back
on itself. As West returns to East, so the dream of a peaceable kingdom in which man and nature might live in harmony under
God's blessing redounds into a nightmare image of impending
apocalypse, "a night scene by El Greco," as Nick imagines it. In
this surreal comment that epitomizes Nick's experience of West
Egg, natural abundance has been transformed into artificial
wealth, envisaged in the figure of a drunken woman carried on a
stretcher by four men in dress suits, her dangling hand "sparkles
cold with jewels. Gravely the men turn in at a house – the wrong
house. But no one knows the woman's name, and no one cares"
(p. 178). The commodity that should sustain and nurture community has been turned inward to engorge the self, to feed a narcis-
sistic oblivion that has shattered all human ties. Gatsby's parties
are, in this sense, anti-feasts. They serve as an extended metaphor
for the failure of America to realize itself in nurturing social
forms.

Like the sightless eyes of Dr T. J. Eckleburg which proclaim
the death of vision, these gargantuan orgies are notable for the
absence they illuminate – the lack of any tie but rumor and
curiosity that might bring men and women together in mutual
recognition and sympathy. As Milton Stern points out, it is money
and the hunger for it that is the source of vitality on all social
levels in the book.[42] Just so, do rumor and curiosity parallel the
circulation of money in the quality of social contact they project.
Transient, impersonal and exploitative, rumor and curiosity flow
through the crowd, fragmenting their subjects into consumable,
titillating objects – a line in a newspaper report, a phrase of
speculative gossip. The grotesque imagery of dismemberment
evoked in Wolfsheim's molar cufflinks and Myrtle's torn breast
suggests the state of partial identity – dissociated, divided, frag-
mented into function and use – in which all the characters exist.

There is pathos in Gatsby's oranges and lemons, which arrive
every Friday in crates from a fruiterer in New York and two days
later leave his back door "in a pyramid of pulpless halves." Like
the glazed turkeys and syrupy cordials that grace his banquet and
bar, the fruit is a reminder of that cornucopia of earthly blessings

which now nurtures a social process in which consumption has become its own end.[43] One might say that what Nick describes are festivities in search of a myth – that is, a comprehensive believable fiction which will redefine wealth in terms of values that express a coherent, even sacramental order of meaning. It is therefore patently ironic that what ultimately distinguishes Gatsby from the "foul dust" floating "in the wake of his dreams" is his stubborn if misconceived faith that he has hold of such an order of value in his yearning for Daisy. For he gives the parties only to win her; when she disdains them they are over.

The coarse reality of the West Egg festivities forms a direct contrast to the ideal community *à deux* that Gatsby briefly manages to create. Although this idyll can be linked to similar bracketed moments in the other books we have discussed (community as it ought to be), it is distinguishable from these on two counts. First, Fitzgerald does not dramatize the personal relationship between the lovers. We never see them alone, never learn anything about their experience of each other, the form their meetings and partings actually take. Secondly, and not unrelated to this lacuna, there is the very nature of Gatsby's desire for Daisy, as we know it from the rest of the book. For though he transmutes a common appetite for wealth and success into a transcendental passion, he wants, in effect, to consume Daisy, to have her just as she was five years before by assimilating her life to the form his imagination has conceived for it. Emerson's conviction that men cannot be much to one another because "Every man is an infinitely repellent orb, and holds his individual being on that condition,"[44] proves itself in Gatsby's version of "individual being." For Gatsby's ideal is conceived in terms that are antithetical to that reciprocity of feeling which is the base of all authentic efforts toward community. Ultimately, his vision becomes a mode of ingestion, patterned on the meretricious social order which sustains it.[45]

As the American upper-class princess whose hypnotic voice is full of both warm human magic and money, Daisy is a kind of fallen culture idol. The nineteenth-century convention which exalted the American girl as an emblem of the moral health of the nation, purifying the culture of all but ennobling sentiments, is travestied here in a reversion to woman's age-old role as temptress and corrupter.[46] While Nick likens her to a silver idol, Gatsby continues to see Daisy only in terms of the former convention. To him, her inherited wealth appears as a kind of natural grace showered on the American upper class. It was a concurrent cultural idea that "wealth is moral . . . riches advertise their owner as a man of character."[47] It is as if, with Daisy as an icon set high "above the hot struggles of the poor" (p. 150), Gatsby might be made truly invulnerable.

Given her significance for Gatsby (and by implication for her author) it is no wonder that Fitzgerald was not able to imagine a love scene between these two, as he once wrote in a letter to H. L. Mencken.[48] To do so would have been to give Daisy an independent moral life that might challenge and confront Gatsby's own. It would have been, perhaps, to give us an image of just that bond of community based in mutual recognition and sympathy which Hawthorne allows Hester and Arthur in the forest and Mark Twain develops between Huck and Jim on the raft. But how could such an interchange be conceptualized in a book whose hero is revered for the exalted singularity of his ideal? Nick, who bemoans the faithlessness of all the others, never sees the likeness between Gatsby's self-absorption and theirs. However acutely attuned to nuances of social decency he is, his awareness does not generate any positive social vision. For himself, Nick remains committed to a self-sufficient solitude that mirrors Gatsby's own.

It is no wonder then that the culminating image of absent community should be that of Gatsby's sparse, rainsoaked funeral, to which Daisy sends no token. While the lack of mourners at his last rites testifies to the futility of Gatsby's dream and the human indifference of an entire society, it also becomes the mark of his special status. His unacknowledged death makes him all the more the outcast hero or god in disguise. For Nick, Gatsby's death transmutes all the tawdry glitter of his life. As anonymous at his funeral as he was at his parties, his death has a purifying function: it establishes Nick's sense of him as a prophet in the wilderness – loyal to a vision of self whose power transcends the corrupt means available to give it form. But is it so surprising, after all, that save for Owl-eyes (who sees what others miss) Gatsby's guests are no more able to perceive themselves in him than he was able to see himself in them? For while Nick indicts them for their cruel dismissal of him in death, the very nature of Gatsby's vision enforces the sense of singularity and mutual separation to which his empty funeral attests.

Among all the novels discussed here, Fitzgerald's presents us with the most comprehensive dramatization of the Emersonian hero in a fallen world. Surely, the novel's power lies in its ability to make us share Nick's viewpoint – to believe in Gatsby as we believe in our own dreams – even as we disapprove of him. But given the acute criticism to which Gatsby's aspirations are subject, we might expect some melioration or resolution of this tension in the ending. Yet with all the benefit of hindsight and history, Nick, our surrogate, can no more free himself of his romantic pessimism than he can lay Gatsby's ghost to rest. The latter's death becomes the pretext for Nick's own withdrawal from human connection. His move West, described as a retreat from "privileged glimpses into the human heart" (p. 2) is also a rejection of that mutual sympathy which is the only real liberation from the wheel of endless longing and endless failure that Nick insists is our inevitable American fate.

Conclusion: *Moby-Dick* and Our Problem with History

The works we have examined significantly resemble one another. Alike in their resistance to the reality of history, each ultimately sanctions an evasion of the pressure of experience upon the shape of American identity.

"My Kinsman, Major Molineux" was published in 1832, when America was a provincial nation with a largely agrarian economy; when much of it was still wilderness; and when political debate over 'universal' suffrage referred to the extension of the vote to property-less white adult males. *The Great Gatsby* was published in 1925, nearly one hundred years later. In the interval America grew into a world power and 'universal' suffrage was revised to include (at least in theory) the entire adult population, regardless of race and gender. That these changes were the issue of a turbulent history – a mixed record of complex social accommodation and profound human injustice – makes all the more paradoxical (and ominous) the evasion of the past, as a personal as well as symbolic motif, by the protagonists of these works. For at bottom, these books all reflect their authors' deep consciousness of that historical drama in which their protagonists inevitably bear a role. As each work comments upon the continuing power of the American dream of a regenerate self to define our experience and determine our moral stance, so each reveals the extent to which this idealism is itself an historical force, encouraging us to conflate the variegated desires of the private self with the redemptive aspirations of the nation.

Indeed, the dichotomous structure of these works suggests just how complex their awareness of historical exigencies may be. Of the four writers I have discussed, Hawthorne, Mark Twain, and Fitzgerald are most recognizably at odds with themselves over the direction and evaluation of historical imperatives. James, who was perhaps the most highly-developed literary artist of his or our century, seeking to persuade us that Strether has won more than he has lost, manages to camouflage the fault lines of history within the landscape of his larger artistic vision. Nevertheless, as we have seen, even he cannot entirely disperse the evidence of human loss at the site where historical contradictions erupt.

Given this authorial awareness, it is all the more noteworthy that the visionary aspiration displayed in these books appears, if anything, to harden during the course of the century spanned by their publication. From Hawthorne's protagonists through Fitzgerald's, there seem to be no signs of a rapprochement between the claims of the 'utopian' self for freedom from human bonds and limitations and the actualities of individual and social existence. Robin's divorce from the past, with its concomitant dissociation from inner complexities, prefigures with remarkable accuracy both the misanthropy of Nick Carraway and the hypertrophied condition of Jay Gatsby, who separates himself not only from his real origins but from all history – that is, from the mess of human entanglements which will always defeat the faith that reality is malleable to one's vision of it.

Indeed, if we were to key this phenomenon to the advance of American imperialism and the increasing secularization and reification of the spiritual dream, we might also note that the stalemate imposed by the geopolitics of the past thirty years has produced a literature which in its displaced, self-devouring energies seems to bear the melancholic imprint of Gatsby's shadow double. There is a line that extends from Nick's impotent retreat into a lost world of childhood forward to the ethos in those works by Salinger, Cheever, Mailer, Updike, and even Roth, which, like Nick himself, continue to reflect a bitter disdain for American actuality and a lingering nostalgia for something other, some lost alternative to the contemporary American scene. Yet, *mutatis mutandis*, we may note that in their search for imaginative or spiritual renewal, these writers circle back to the traditional sacraments of nineteenth-century romanticism and the romantic decadence – the immanence of nature, the intuitions of childhood, the ambiguities of the haunted, self-reflecting mind, the intoxications of compulsive fornication, criminality and madness.

But, as Michael Rogin has demonstrated, in its specifically political sense the impact of American imperialism on our writers is not a phenomenon restricted to the present century or the current age.[1] At the start of the period spanned by this study, there is one work which responds directly to the ideology of American power. *Moby-Dick* offers a prescient, if not prophetic, account of the trajectory of American moral ambition in heady alliance with the mercantile energies of an expansionist nation. Yet for all the narrator's complex criticism of the imperative that drives Ahab onward, the ending returns us to that very wilderness of ideal possibility which has nurtured Ahab's delusive vision.

Melville's response to the public scene, his bitter consciousness of the difference between the exigencies of historical reality and the illusory longing for moral absolutes, frees neither him nor us from the compulsion to escape the restrictions of the "slavish shore" in the quest for a redemptive homeland still to be. Ishmael's final reassertion of his "orphan" status – the last word of the book – recalls his observation upon first putting out from New Bedford that "one most perilous and long voyage ended, only begins a second . . . and so on for ever"[2]. In *Moby-Dick* the ideal so overpowers the real that there is no room for an accommodation, no dialectic at all between them. In its manifold treatment of American aspiration wedded to the realities of American political and economic life, Melville's narrative allows us to gauge even more clearly the weight of our cultural predispositions. In so doing, it elucidates the relation between visionary energy and the rejected historical middle ground which has sustained this ambition within our literature, as perhaps within our national life.

While the sinking of the *Pequod*, with the American eagle nailed to its mainmast, serves as lament for the nobility of a national project gone wrong, its end does not end the tale. In informing us how the narrator survived, the epilogue serves as a kind of textual reprise, conflating in its brief paragraph allusions to the story of Job, to the Rachel of the prophet Jeremiah and the gospel of Matthew and, of course, to the biblical status of Abraham's outcast child, Ishmael himself. Throughout the story, the framework of biblical reference reminds us of the historical burden under which not only Ahab, but all hands aboard the *Pequod* sail. The Calvinist cosmology which Ahab challenges is, like the whaling enterprise itself, a specifically American application of an ancient practice or principle with universal significance. Thus, like his country's, Ahab's identity is founded upon a patrimony which, however he may invert its terms, provides him with the moral will to reconceive the purpose and meaning of an ordinary commercial voyage by investing it with the power of his symbolic imagination.

Whether Ahab's rebellion against the creation (as he conceives it) has driven him insane, or whether his insanity has driven him to rebel, is ultimately unknowable. But the mingled strains of his character – harsh, self-righteous, heroically audacious, and brave in the conscious acceptance of his monomania – allow Melville to comment upon both the contemporaneous political manifestations of America's belief in its special destiny and on the grounds of that belief which have influenced and encouraged this national self-conception. Yet Ishmael's equivocal restoration – epitomized in the symbol of the coffin life-buoy – suggests that in his endless wandering, the quest for Moby-Dick may be, after all, only an episode in a larger national-*cum*-universal design.

In assuming the role of Job's messenger ("And I only am escaped to tell thee"), Ishmael implicitly conflates the Job-like protests of Ahab against the arbitrary nature of God's torments with the fate as well as the future prospects of the once-blessed American nation of his readers. Unlike Ahab, Job eventually repents of his rage against God, is redeemed and restored to his former estate. For, again unlike Ahab, Job comes to acknowledge his own limitations. He cannot hook leviathan, much less God. The despairing Job asks "how should man be just with God?" (9:2) and finally acknowledges that God's ways cannot be judged by man's. But neither Ahab nor the crew he has galvanized into following him is redeemed. On the contrary, Ahab, in his refusal to recognize human limits ("I'd strike the sun if it insulted me" [p. 144]) is perhaps a Job whose testing has turned him into God's enemy. As the chase progresses Captain Ahab (his name recalls an apostate Hebrew king of Samaria who worshipped Baal) seduces the crew to his goal by igniting their lust for gold and stirring their ready appetite for violent and vengeful combat. The nearer they get to Moby-Dick, the more dose Ahab himself seem to mirror the image of the enemy he seeks. In this sense, the fate of Ahab and his crew exemplifies the trap which American moral arrogance sets for itself. Ahab's self-assertion has cost him his humanity. Damned by his obsession, he has lost touch with common affections and human needs. Ultimately, it should be emphasized, his rebellion is not only against the God of his Puritan forebears, but against human nature as well.

For Ahab to acknowledge moral complexity in himself as in others, to recognize his own self-projection in the image he creates of the whale, would be to put the whole of his ambitious project into doubt. As Ishmael observes, the awfulness of the sea, the horror at the heart of things, that surrounds man also lies within him. Either in orthodox or transcendental terms, the 'me' and the 'not-me,' spirit and nature are ultimately akin. But Ahab's dark version of "linked analogies" no more acknowledges the complexity of the inner self than does Emerson's cosmic optimism. Ahab's spiritual project thus approximates the cast of mind of a nation whose faith in its high purpose and sacred significance enables it to evade the truths of its own historical character – a faith which in Melville's day was carrying the country headlong toward the catastrophe of the Civil War.

Moreover, the resistance or opposition to Ahab which we might expect from Ishmael or others never materializes. Rather, Ahab's denial of his own nature creates an atmosphere of human isolation and self-preoccupation which seems to blanket the entire ship. Though many individual soliloquies are delivered on board the *Pequod*, there is little genuine conversation or social intercourse among the members of this highly diverse crew. It is "as if each man were caught within his own small space, alone, connected with other men only artificially and by convention."[3] Once on board ship, Ishmael's consciousness of a democratic community, "a common continent of men," remains a shining abstraction rather than an enacted experience with consequences and effects. For just as Ahab is technically guilty of the charge of usurpation in redirecting the purpose of the voyage (p. 184), so he usurps all the conceivable emotional space within the book. Like his Puritan ancestors, he sees his role as exemplary, himself an actor in a cosmic plot. Starbuck's protest against the vengeful hunting of a dumb beast is no match for Ahab's exhortations. On board the *Pequod*, there is no place other than with Ahab for either Ishmael, the crew, or the reader to stand.

Ishmael's sense of life as a formless flux, his celebration of a kind of primal sensuality as the source of human brotherhood, is in such consistent tension with his apprehension of an underlying horror, a "demonism in the world," that it provides a kind of rationale for his paralysis. He may be a "voyaging mind," as Charles Feidelson emphasizes,[4] but he is also a disengaged one. Once he leaves the fellowship of the Spouter Inn and enters upon the wintry open sea, he seems incapable of objectifying his experience by positing any credible alternative to Ahab's vision. Without Ahab's command, in all its senses, there would be no coherence to life on board ship, and the ship serves – as it does regularly in Melville's work – as a metonymy of the relations among men in society at large. Ahab provides not only discipline and order, but a focussed interpretation of experience in an essentially indeterminate and multi-perspectival world. Ironically, or perhaps necessarily, the social middle ground of common affections and circumscribed moral options, where we might expect Ishmael and the others to take a stand against Ahab's usurpation, is depicted as the most dream-like and illusory of all socio-moral possibilities. Indeed Ishmael himself, who is actually absent as a character for long portions of the book, is not only a stand-in for the Melvillean voyaging mind, but also an emblem of that flux of historical consciousness or spirit which has, in effect, inevitably produced Ahab.

Like the other works we have discussed, *Moby-Dick* offers us a dichotomy of moral choices, extremes of action and inaction: either we stand with Ahab in his rigid self-dissociation or we are plunged with Pip into the formless void at the core of things – a void which leads to the terror of ultimate impotence.

The final rescue of Ishmael, the orphan outcast, directly connects him to the remnant of Israel in the book of Jeremiah. There, Rachel, the mother of the Jewish people, weeping for her children "because they were not" (31:15), is promised deliverance: "And thus there is hope in thine end, saith the Lord, that thy children shall come again to their own border" (31:17). It is this imagery of another biblical Zion, to be built on New England soil, which the emigrant Puritans bequeathed to their American descendants, that Melville both alludes to and transmutes in the figure of Ishmael. For like the ancient Hebrews, the American Puritans identified themselves and their vision with Isaac, Abraham's legitimate son, and the patriarch of Israel. Ishmael, the son of Abraham's slavewoman Hagar, was separated from Israel, but promised by God that in the fullness of time his seed would engender another nation. Ishmael stands for unknown possibility. The form and faith of the original dream having failed, Melville, like Ahab, refuses to question the dream itself; instead, he projects another, a nineteenth-century vision, perhaps, of a more inclusively democratic brotherhood. For the inter-racial 'marriage' of Quee-queg and Ishmael, two social outcasts who together embody a more humane version of self-reliance than that of the 'dictator' Captain Ahab, may provide some sort of ideal pattern. Yet, at the end, Ishmael is further than ever from that shared sense of human connection than he was at the start of the story.

Nothing in our experience of *Moby-Dick* provides us with any hope that such a direction is actually conceivable. For without the force of Ahab's will the international crew of the *Pequod* is only a collection of "mongrel renegades [and] . . . castaways;" while the mates, who are American, are little more than "morally enfeebled" functionaries. Viewed organically, the process of accul-turation which produces American individualism seems to offer little social hope. Yet, the *Rachel* continues to search for her lost children and Ishmael for his ideal homeland.

Ishmael's wanderings link him to a tradition of emigration from the constraints of the past – from an old and time-burdened world – that is one of the formative themes of our national experience. Nick travels east, Strether and Hester cross the Atlantic, Huck flees to the river, and by virtue of these actions each stands on the threshold of a new consciousness of self and social possibility. Yet for each protagonist this consciousness proves stillborn. What starts as a vision of new freedom ends in a *cul de sac* of old truths and binding forces. In effect, the world they flee moves with them; reconstituted in a more radical form, it turns out to be only a variant of the one left behind. And though the protagonist's resist-ance becomes the measure of his autonomous consciousness, each, in his needs and nature – by virtue, ironically, of his representative role – inevitably bears the stamp of the world he resists. Thus it becomes necessary in the end to take flight from that part of the self that belongs to history – whether it be dramatized as the tyranny of a socialized conscience, the capitulation to social forces, or the responsibilities owed to another human being – if the capacity for vision is to be conserved.

It is this necessity that accounts, I believe, for that sense of human impoverishment, a dissolution of the normal contours of self, which haunts the Ishmael-like characters in American fiction and defines their fate in the end. In addition to those considered here, one thinks of Lily Bart in *The House of Mirth* and Undine Spragg in *The Custom of the Country*, of Carrie and Hurstwood in *Sister Carrie*, and Jake Barnes in *The Sun Also Rises*. Each suffers from an emotional emptiness or impotence – a condition which seems as much a function of their designated status, or symbolic role, within the narrative structure as a problem of individual character. Moreover, although the malady is related to the social and historical circumstances which pertain to each character, it is as consistent as is their common ability to discard the consequences of the past and to establish themselves in a mental space beyond the reach of memory. But, as Hans Myerhoff has emphasized, what sense of self we possess is dependent upon fragments of memory, dependent upon our continuous connection and interrelationship with moments of past time, out of which we construct and redefine our personal authenticity.[5] Though memory is notoriously fragile and delusive and history not synonymous with identity, the interconnection between these dual expressions of consciousness (individual and social) surely provides the ground upon which any coherent sense of identity is built. But since, in these American works, flight or its variants (including economic, aesthetic, and spiritual upward mobility) substitutes for the process of self-encounter or social confrontation, we are left without roots from which either identity or its social correlative, community might grow. Instead, identity becomes allied to the postponed vision and so has the paradoxical effect of insuring that the ideal community which has failed to emerge, never will emerge.

Unlike his European cousin whose identity is shaped in the crucible of society, the American hero's identity depends upon a vision of self which precedes and resists the definition experience would impose upon him. For the American hero, being true to one's vision is being a self. Nothing else seems required. Indeed, the prospect of immersion in social experience, with its potential for moral confusion, self-exposure, and self-doubt, produces a response that often borders on terror, or periodically explodes in scorn and disgust. Society as it appears in each of the books discussed is not only a contaminating and corrupting presence but represents (as it does overtly in "My Kinsman, Major Molineux") the darkest, most repellent side of human nature. The mocking cruelty of the Boston revolutionaries that Robin witnesses is matched by the qualities of the shore inhabitants whom Huck encounters. And for Strether, the world on both sides of the Atlantic reverberates with echoes of the jungle. Gloriani's guests have the fascination of glossy beasts. Beneath her fine manners and exalted feelings, Mrs Newsome, like her daughter, is a predator. Though they wear their fur "the smooth side out . . . [and] don't lash about and shake the cage, . . . they always get there" (pp. 215–16). In these books, a loving community is what might have been, what ought to be; society is the all-too-fearsome reality.

The barbarities of the social world thus serve as both motive and justification for the hero's withdrawal. But what he evades is any correspondence to aspects of his own nature. By blinking away this truth, falling asleep in the face of it, or closing the door on it (as Robin, Huck, and Strether do), the self-integration that depends upon a dialectical struggle with the Other is denied. Instead, these heroes evade challenge by absorbing the present into their transcendent hopes and dreams. Hester looks forward to the revelation of "a new truth" that will alter the relations of men and women; Gatsby remains faithful to the green light blinking at the end of Daisy's dock; Strether holds fast to his "wonderful impressions"; and Huck turns the lawlessness of the actual western territory into a metaphoric equivalent of natural goodness.

The human cost of this mode of incorporation is great. For it results not in a more generous and inclusive response to experience, as we might wish to think, but in its opposite: a narrow asceticism, or a defensive exclusion of complexity, or simply a retreat in the face of human suffering. (It is worth reminding ourselves that *Pierre* and "Bartleby," with their emphatic regression into stony silence, directly followed *Moby-Dick*.) To preserve his visionary identity the hero must separate one part of himself from another, must commit himself to a little death – or, in Gatsby's case, to an actual one – in order to maintain the only version of self that seems real to him.

Ursula Brumm, in discussing the meaning of the wilderness to the American Puritans, defines it as not only a place where they could establish their own congregations according to their own standards, but one that seemed free from the corruptions of history; the place where, despite temptations, "God leads those for whom he has something special in store." Despite the historical accomplishment of the settlements, says Brumm, there is a continuing "connection between Nonconformity and wilderness, between people of pure belief and land of uncorrupted nature." The Nonconformist must, metaphorically speaking, "co-exist with the wilderness forever."[6] But to co-exist with the wilderness is continually to dissolve the binding ties of historical circumstance. It is to turn reality into so artificial or ephemeral a construct that it can be severed at will from the 'true' or 'authentic' self which remains inviolable within. We can now see how the pattern which underlies these novels ends in a vicious circle. As long as identity is predicated on an ideal, history is the enemy that must be defined as a polar opposite in order to regenerate and sustain an antithetical vision.

The logic of this duality perhaps accounts for the extremely restrictive structure of these books. Choices are minimal; relations condensed; and the interiority of the characters, even in the Jamesian drama of consciousness, a highly limited and controlled affair. Yet one of the merits of this structure is that it intensifies the pull of the hero's divided sympathies – his attraction toward that world whose failed possibilities he can neither truly confront nor forgive. Huck longs for the lighted windows of the shore; Strether delights in the "warm circle of life" represented by Miss Gostrey's "things"; Nick is dazzled and bemused by life's "inexhaustible variety"; and the narrator of *Moby-Dick* devotes two-thirds of his work to the resonant realities of whaling. In these novels, the fascination of the actual provides as much vitality as does the hero's alternative vision.

Finally, this tension returns us to the point with which we began: the use of our authors' historical consciousness. For the past as both theme and/or setting is, of course, intrinsic to each of these works. More than symbolizing a lost or betrayed sense of freedom, the past functions to emphasize the futility of the search. Hawthorne's novel is the only one that actually deals with this past as history, as a collection of events that have a specific relation to time and place. But as we noted earlier, his scene involves fusions and abstractions; in *The Scarlet Letter* the past has generic meaning. It conflates the historical beginnings of the country with the biblical Fall – the entry of our first parents into the wilderness of the world. In this sense Hawthorne's use of the past is similar to that of the other authors. For to enter or seek to recapture this lost past is, as we see again and again, only to encounter another version of the present. In each of these books the lesson is the same: what is lost was lost at the beginning; the well is poisoned at the source.

Hawthorne puts it most conclusively – it is his essential subject: as long as the wilderness is co-extensive with the human heart, utopian hopes will be subject to its terrors, needs, and limitations. Fitzgerald, who was, perhaps, closest to Hawthorne in his concern with the social texture of historical truth, reminds us through the image of the Dutch sailors gazing at the "fresh, green breast of the new world" that this wonder is forever connected with the experience of transit – before the forest is cleared; before the human adventurer puts his foot on the shore and encounters himself in the act of settlement. Strether announces in the midst of his re-awakening, "What one loses one loses; make no mistake about that . . ." And Mark Twain, by stressing the obverse side of this American desire – the obsession with motion and flight – testifies to the same truth.

However far back in time or space we go, we find the same longing and the same loss. The desire for a new world will, no doubt, always be with us: perhaps it is a necessary and enlivening human hope. But when this aspiration is maintained at the cost of self-recognition, as it is in the American version, we doom ourselves to wander forever, like Hester, within the circuit of the same dismal maze. These books provide us with extraordinarily compelling images of our own aspirations as well as their pitfalls and traps. Our authors have done their work. It is to ourselves we must look, to the value of our own commitments and loyalties, if we are ever to break free of this cycle.

Notes

1. Frank Kermode, *The Sense of an Ending* (New York, Oxford Univ. Press, 1967), p. 44. Plots rely on turning ordinary, successive, and humanly meaningless time into moments of charged meaning. *Chronos* becomes *kairos*: "a point in time filled with significance . . . derived from its relation to the end."

2. For a discussion of Shakespeare's use of the Bermuda Pamphlets and other voyaging materials see Frank Kermode's introduction to the Arden Edition of *The Tempest* (London, Methuen, 1964), pp. xxv–xxxiv. For an examination of the traditional European world view challenged by the "discovery" of America, see Edmund O'Gorman, *The Invention of America* (Bloomington, Indiana Univ. Press, 1961).

3. *The Sense of an Ending*, p. 29.

4. See Robert M. Adams, *Strains of Discord: Studies in Literary Openness* (Ithaca, Cornell Univ. Press, 1958); Alan Friedman, *The Turn of the Novel* (New York, Oxford Univ. Press, 1966); Marianna Torgovnick, *Closure in the Novel* (Princeton, Princeton Univ. Press, 1981).

5. Clifford Geertz, *The Interpretation of Cultures* (New York, Basic Books, 1973), p. 35.

6. *Ibid.*, pp. 44, 49.

7. For an historical overview of American millennialism see Ernst Tuveson, *Redeemer Nation* (Chicago, Univ. of Chicago Press, 1968), and especially p. 205.

8. Notable among those critics who have stressed the centrality of Emerson's cultural role are several whose work has had a particular influence on this study: Quentin Anderson, *The Imperial Self* (New York, Vintage, 1971); Richard Poirier, *A World Elsewhere* (New York, Oxford Univ. Press, 1966); Sacvan Bercovitch, *The Puritan Origins of the American Self* (New Haven, Yale Univ. Press, 1975).

9. Cf. Harold Bloom, *New York Review of Books* (Nov. 22, 1984), pp. 19–24. See also F. O. Matthiessen, *American Renaissance* (New York, Oxford Univ. Press, 1941); R. W. B. Lewis, *The American Adam* (Chicago, Univ. of Chicago Press, 1955).

10. But notwithstanding his own rejection of the "sepulchres of the fathers," Emerson is clearly part of a tradition of radical self-

assertion which, from one perspective, can itself be considered a central strain of American historical experience – reaching from Ann Hutchinson and Roger Williams, through Thomas Paine and Thomas Jefferson. As Sacvan Bercovitch has shown, however, Emerson feared the self-isolation of European-style antinomianism and so redefined it in terms of the Puritan conception of mission that runs from Mather through Edwards and "interweaves personal and corporate self-fulfillment." Emerson's contribution is exemplary because it involves a melding of spiritual, moral, and political strains of American experience into a visionary, albeit sectarian-free, conception of the new man. "The rhetoric he inherited enabled him to dissolve all differences between history and the self . . . by revealing himself as the representative American." *Puritan Origins*, pp. 169, 173.

11. *Selections from Ralph Waldo Emerson*, ed. Stephen Whicher (Boston, Riverside Press, 1960), p. 50.

12. *Ibid.*, p. 56.

13. *Puritan Origins*, pp. 165, 169.

14. Whicher, p. 79.

15. Whicher, p. 24.

16. F. O. Matthiessen, *American Renaissance* (New York, Oxford Univ. Press, 1941), p. 179.

17. See Helen W. Papashvily, *All the Happy Endings* (New York, Harper & Bros., 1956).

18. Henry James, *The Golden Bowl* (New York, Dell, 1963), p. 511.

19. Cf. Robert Scholes and Robert Kellogg, *The Nature of Narrative* (London, Oxford Univ. Press, 1966), p. 82. "Meaning, in a work of narrative art, is a function of the relationship between two worlds: the fictional world created by the author and the 'real' world, the apprehendable universe. When we say we 'understand' a narrative we mean that we have found a satisfactory relationship or set of relationships between these two worlds."

20. Lionel Trilling, "An American View of English Literature," in *Speaking of Literature and Society* (New York, Harcourt, Brace, Jovanovich, 1980), pp. 263, 265.

21. Preface to *The Marble Faun* (New York, NAL, 1961), p. vi.

22. D. H. Lawrence, *Studies in Classic American Literature*, 1923 (rpt. New York, Viking, 1964), p. 7.

23. *A World Elsewhere*, pp. 206–7.

24. *A World Elsewhere*, pp. 6–7. "Works like *Moby-Dick* or *The Ambassadors* . . . are designed to make the reader feel that his ordinary world has been acknowledged, even exhaustively, only to be dispensed with as a source of moral or psychological standards . . . their extravagances of language are an exultation in the exercise of consciousness momentarily set free."

25. Leslie A. Fiedler, *Love and Death in the American Novel* (New

York, Stein and Day, 1966). The entire book explicates this thesis, but a representative section would be its treatment of *Huckleberry Finn*, pp. 269–90.

26. Sacvan Bercovitch, in *The American Jeremiad* (Madison, Univ. of Wisconsin Press, 1978), has defined the form in contradistinction to the traditional European one. While the traditional mode laments the ways of the world and a depraved humanity, the American Puritans "sounded a different note." Believing themselves to be agents of "a sacred historical design," they inverted the "doctrine of vengeance into a promise of ultimate success." Bercovitch sees the jeremiad persisting "throughout the eighteenth and nineteenth centuries in all forms of literature" (pp. 8, 7, 11). Cf. especially the comment that "the movement [of *The Scarlet Letter*] is remarkably similar to that of the jeremiad" (p. 207).

27. Cf. Bercovitch's discussion of Emersonian self-reliance in *Puritan Origins*, p. 176. "It [self-reliance] is the consummate expression of a culture which places an immense premium on independence while denouncing all forms of eccentricity and elitism. . . . The self-reliant American . . . remains by definition the hero as guide and national benefactor."

CHAPTER I

Nathaniel Hawthorne: "My Kinsman, Major Molineux": The Several Voices of Independence

1. First published in *The Token*, 1832. All references here are to *The Centenary Edition of the Works of Nathaniel Hawthorne*, Vol. XI (Columbus, Ohio State Univ. Press, 1962–8) and hereafter included in parentheses in the text.

2. Michael Colacurcio, *The Province of Piety: Moral History in Hawthorne's Early Tales* (Cambridge, Harvard Univ. Press, 1984), believes that Hawthorne deliberately ran together two rather different historical moments in eighteenth-century political life in order to stress the theme of mob violence as an antidote to the popular view of the Revolution as holy history, p. 136.

3. In his discussion, cited above, Michael Colacurcio claims that the tale actually resists a too-easy conflation of individual "coming of age" with proto-revolutionary experience; that Robin has "merely bungled his way to the center of an action entirely independent of his personal anxieties" (*ibid.*, p. 141). But this view is predicated on assumptions about the nature of individual Oedipal experience which seem unduly restrictive.

Colacurcio claims that since the story is primarily directed against the contemporary myth of the Revolution as a calm and stately event, its focus on a "minor mob scene" as epitome is designed to make Robin's coming-of-age merely coincidental with the evening's events. But it seems more in keeping with the tale's complex semantics to view it as a re-vision of what coming-of-age means in a revolutionary climate. A break with one's parent, as the Revolution was popularly conceived to be, is not ordinarily the same thing as parricide, but under certain conditions and pressures the abnormal illuminates the "normal," since at the root they are indeed entwined. From whence do historical actions emanate and who is their ultimate agent if not the individual?

4. Peter Shaw, *American Patriots and the Rituals of Revolution* (Cambridge, Harvard Univ. Press, 1981), p. 211, has suggested that Robin's name derives from Robin Hood, who was a figure of sacrifice, a Frazerean scapegoat in the English festival tradition, and thus a fertility deity. Michael Colacurcio has linked the name to English politics through the "Robinocracy" of "Robin" Walpole, p. 140. While the antecedent game has its fascinations and potential enrichments, in this instance, at least, it only serves to gild the more obvious significance which the story itself provides.

5. See Peter Shaw, "Fathers and Sons, And the Ambiguities of the Revolution in 'My Kinsman, Major Molineux,'" *New England Quarterly* 49 (1976), p. 560. Shaw emphasizes the ritual significance of the story and points out that "for hundreds of years governments based their legitimacy on rituals that enacted the king-father analogy and emphasized the identification of all officials with the king as father."

6. Bier, "Weberism, Franklin, and the Transcendental Style," *NEQ*, 43 (6, 1970) pp. 179–92; Gilmore, "Emerson and the Persistence of the Commodity," *Harvard English Studies*, #10, ed. Joel Porte (Cambridge, Harvard Univ. Press, 1982), pp. 65–84.

7. Colacurcio p. 135.

8. For another view of this phenomenon see Sacvan Bercovitch, "The Puritan Errand Reassessed," in *Toward a New American Literary History* (Durham, Duke Univ. Press, 1980).

9. Colacurcio, like Robert Lowell, whom he cites, concludes that the guide is the minister of the South Church and identifies him as Charles Chauncey, who was a member of the Black Regiment and engaged in various mob actions, p. 569, n. 97. This information only further supports one's sense that Robin's guide serves as a moral as well as political tutor; and that his role is both to lead and reassure. For, however we may choose to shade it with irony, his voice counts in our assessment of Robin's character.

10. See David Levin, *History as Romantic Art* (rpt. New York, Harcourt, Brace and World, 1963), pp. 24, 27 esp.
11. Colacurcio, p. 152.
12. Morgan, *The Challenge of the American Revolution* (New York, Norton & Co., 1976), p. 109. For a description of the European political climate at this time, see E. J. Hobsbawm, *The Age of Revolution 1789–1848* (New York, NAL, 1962), p. 137 and foll.
13. By social myth I mean a narrative that is repeatedly retold, or reread, as a means of reinforcing those values which exemplify a culture's distinctive solution to problems of identity. For a judicious discussion of the problematics of myth see G. S. Kirk, *Myth: Its Meaning and Functions in Ancient and Other Cultures* (Berkeley, Univ. of California Press, 1970).
14. *Autobiography*, ed. Larabee et al. (New Haven, Yale Univ. Press, 1904), p. 75.
15. See Bruno Bettleheim, *The Uses of Enchantment* (New York, Knopf, 1976), for an extended examination of the therapeutic function of fairy tales.
16. For the fullest exploration of the ritual possibilities connected to the name Molineux, see Peter Shaw, *American Patriots*. William Molineux led a proto-revolutionary uprising in Boston, in 1768, against Thomas Hutchinson's house; later, he was threatened by such a crowd himself when he retreated from militancy. Shaw sees the use of the name here as an example of Hawthorne's wish to enact "a kind of expiation for the American Revolution's sins of excess," p. 190.
17. *A World Elsewhere*, p. 113.
18. Lesser, "The Image of the Father," *Partisan Review*, 22 (Summer, 1955), pp. 370–90.
19. Yehoshua Arieli, *Individualism and Nationalism in American Ideology* (Cambridge, Harvard Univ. Press, 1964), p. 193.
20. Joseph Conrad, *Lord Jim* (New York, Penguin, 1975), p. 163.

CHAPTER II

Bleak Dreams: Restriction and Aspiration in *The Scarlet Letter*

1. For an extended discussion of this symbolism see the following: Hyatt Howe Waggoner, *Hawthorne: A Critical Study* (Cambridge, MA, The Belknap Press, 1955); Harry Levin, *The Power of Blackness: Hawthorne, Poe and Melville* (New York, Alfred A. Knopf, Inc., 1958). Relevant sections of each are reprinted in *The Scarlet Letter*, ed. Bradley, Beatty, and Long (New York, Norton Critical Edition, 1961), pp. 308–17; 350–8. Hereafter cited as Norton Critical.
2. Nathaniel Hawthorne, *The Scarlet Letter*, pub. 1850 (rpt. New

York, Norton Critical Ed., 1961) p. 38. All quotations will be from this edition and page numbers hereafter included in parentheses in the text.

3. Cf. Richard Brodhead, *Hawthorne, Melville, and the Novel* (Chicago, Univ of Chicago Press, 1975), p. 52. "Characters, under the burden of their situation, come to dehumanize themselves even more thoroughly than their oppressors do."

4. Cf. Yehoshua Arieli, *Individualism and Nationalism in American Ideology*, p. 275. Arieli traces the ideological origins of American individualism, which, in the nineteenth century, he finds becomes the basis for a reinterpretation of democracy. It is individualism which links the Puritan mission with the various social reform movements of the 1830s and 40s. "Abolition, education, temperance, women's rights . . . experiments in the reorganization of society . . . were all the legitimate offspring of radical Unitarian and transcendental perfection . . . the idea of America as the kingdom of God, as the realization of absolutely valid ethical, spiritual, and social values, was predominant. Such ideals of national identification were incompatible with the acknowledgement of historically formed rights and the sovereignty of a state based on popular consent. . . . The revolt in the name of a higher law was a revolt of the American ideal against the American reality"; a faith that the route to social Utopia lay in the "spiritual and moral power" of the regenerate individual.

5. Cf. her remarks to Chillingworth on his relating that the magistrates might be ready to remove the letter: "Where I worthy to be quit of it, it would fall away of its own nature, or be transformed into something that should speak a different purport" (p. 122).

6. *Puritan Origins of the American Self*, p. 177.

7. For the response to the book in Hawthorne's day, see Bertha Faust, *Hawthorne's Contemporaneous Reputation*, 1939 (rpt. New York, Octagon Books, Inc., 1968), esp. pp. 79, 82. Influential and representative views in this century include those of D. H. Lawrence, *Studies in Classic American Literature* (rpt. New York, Viking, 1964), pp. 83–100; Henry James, *Hawthorne* (London, 1879); Hyatt Howe Waggoner, *Hawthorne*; Roy Male, *Hawthorne's Tragic Vision* (New York, Norton, 1964); Harry Levin, *The Power of Blackness*, and R. W. B. Lewis, *The American Adam* (Chicago, Univ. of Chicago Press, 1955), pp. 110–26.

8. *The Imperial Self*, pp. 61, 81.

9. See *Puritan Origins of the American Self*, pp. 136–86.

10. "Reality in America," *The Liberal Imagination* (New York, Doubleday Anchor, 1950), p. 7. "A culture is not a flow . . . the form of its existence is struggle, or at least debate – it is nothing

if not a dialectic. And in any culture there are likely to be certain artists who contain a large part of the dialectic within themselves, their meaning and power lying in their contradictions."

11. John Winthrop, "A Model of Christian Charity," quoted in Perry Miller, *Errand into the Wilderness* (New York, Harper Torchbooks, 1956), p. 12.

12. See Michael Colacurcio's discussion of "Young Goodman Brown" and "The Minister's Block Veil" in *The Province of Piety*.

13. See prec. chapter.

14. Frederic Carpenter, *American Literature and the American Dream* (New York, Philosophical Library, 1955), rpt. Norton Critical, pp. 284–93.

15. Alexis de Tocqueville, *Democracy in America*, ed. Phillips Bradley (New York, Vintage Books, 1945), Vol. II, p. 117.

16. Cf. Mark Van Doren, *Nathaniel Hawthorne* (New York, William Sloane, Assoc., 1949), pp. 150–4.

17. This is a point Sacvan Bercovitch has made about the endings of many American novels.

CHAPTER III

Mark Twain's Great Evasion: *Adventures of Huckleberry Finn*

1. Pub. in England, Dec., 1884; U.S., Feb., 1885. Thomas Sergeant Perry, in the earliest signed American review, anticipated many later critics in remarking that where truthfulness gives way to "ingenious invention" the book suffers. *Century*, 1 (May, 1885). Rpt. Bradley, Beatty *et al.*, eds. Norton Authoritative Text and Criticism (New York, 1977), pp. 289–90.

2. For two opposing views of Huck's character, representative of the range of attempts to account formally for the ending, see Richard P. Adams, "The Unity and Coherence of *Huckleberry Finn*," *Tulane Studies in English*, VI (1956), pp. 87–102; Martha Banta, "Rebirth or Revenge: The Endings of *Huckleberry Finn* and *The American*," *Modern Fiction Studies*, XV (Summer, 69), pp. 191–207. Adams notes that critical attention to the text began with Lionel Trilling's introduction to the Rinehart edition (1948), in which he defended the ending on formal and thematic grounds. Previously, it had been generally deplored. Trilling's essay can be found in *The Liberal Imagination* (New York, Anchor, 1950).

3. For a recent summary of these arguments see Brook Thomas, "*The House of the Seven Gables*: Reading the Romance of America" *PMLA*, vol. 97, no. 2 (March, 1982), pp. 195–211.

4. There is a suggestive historical irony in the fact that although

Huck never achieves status within his own novel, he, far more than Hester, has now become a figure of cultural myth – both in the 'popular mind' and in the scholarly and critical commentary that has burgeoned since World War II. For a useful perspective on this, see Alan Trachtenberg, "The form of Freedom in *The Adventures of Huckleberry Finn*," *Southern Review*, N.S. VI (Oct., 1970), pp. 954–71. Trachtenberg points out that after the Second World War Huck was regularly taken for an image of wise innocence in a corrupt world, "natural man achieving independence in a depraved society." But this criticism "should be understood in light of the political and social anxieties of the postwar period"; for the question of freedom, Huck's and Jim's both, remains unresolved in the novel (p. 955).

5. 'Mark Twain,' *The Southern Review*, N.S. VIII (July, 1970), no. 3, pp. 459–93.

6. Cf. Amy Lang, "The Antinomian Strain in American Culture," unpub. dissertation, Columbia University (1980). She demonstrates that American antinomianism has a profoundly conservative aspect. By stressing dependence upon "the inner motion of the heart" as the only means to truth, it avoids social and political conflict altogether; thus making "human effort futile and unnecessary" (p. 123). Moreover, what appears as individual resistance is actually a mode of incorporation, in which the "individual quest and national progress mirror one another" (p. 166).

7. Leo Marx, "Mr. Eliot, Mr. Trilling, and *Huckleberry Finn*," *American Scholar* (Aut., 1953), pp. 423–40. See also Bernard DeVoto, *Mark Twain at Work* (1942; reissue, Boston, Houghton Mifflin Co., 1967), p. 91; and Ernest Hemingway, *The Green Hills of Africa* (New York, Scribners, 1935), p. 22. "You must stop where the Nigger Jim is stolen from the boys [sic]. That is the real end. The rest is just cheating."

8. Cf. DeVoto, *Mark Twain at Work*, p. 92. Based on his reading of Twain's unpublished papers, DeVoto believed that he was ignorant of the change of tone in the ending and its effect on the reader; that he wrote "in response to an inner drive, consequently exercised little voluntary control over and [was] unable to criticize what he had written." Many later critics have contested this description of Twain's artistry; see especially, Walter Blair, *Mark Twain and Huck Finn* (Berkeley, Univ. of Calif. Press, 1960); although Blair, too, is confounded by the tone of the ending.

9. Justin Kaplan, *Mr. Clemens and Mark Twain* (New York, Simon and Schuster, 1966), pp. 211, 206.

10. Lionel Trilling, concerned to save the ending for the book, and thus to reinforce Huck's value as a moral perceiver, accepted

Huck's submissiveness to Tom as characteristic of his innate modesty. But this view completely overlooks, as do many subsequent refutations of it, what I believe should be the principal consideration here; i.e., the gratuitous humiliation of Jim and Huck. For Trilling's discussion, see *The Liberal Imagination*, pp. 100–13.

11. Sigmund Freud, *Jokes and Their Relation to the Unconscious*, trans. and ed., James Strachey (New York, W. W. Norton Co., Inc., 1960), p. 29 & *passim*.

12. For backwoods humor see DeVoto, *Mark Twain's America* (1932; reissue, Boston, Houghton Mifflin Co., 1967); and Kenneth Lynn, *Mark Twain and Southwestern Humor* (Boston, Little Brown & Co., 1959). On the analogy with dreams, the reader should be reminded here of Robin Molineux's similarly bewildered state.

13. On the failure of Reconstruction as the satiric motive for this episode, see Richard and Rita Gollin, "*Huck Finn* and the Time of the Evasion," *Modern Language Studies*, 9, ii (Spring, 1979), pp. 5–15.

14. *Adventures of Huckleberry Finn*, ed. Henry Nash Smith (Boston, Riverside Edition, 1958), p. 208. All citations will be from this edition and, hereafter, page numbers will be included in text.

15. Walter Blair records that throughout the writing of *Huckleberry Finn*, Mark Twain was reading W. E. H. Lecky's *History of European Morals*. Blair found in Twain's marginalia and notebooks a wavering between the two major views of man that Lecky discussess: i.e., motivated by intuitive powers of goodness or driven by exterior forces and selfish interests. Just before Mark Twain wrote the concluding parts "he delivered a paper in which he championed determinism and selfish motivation." Furthermore, Twain's marginalia show that he recognized that moral influences and perceptions begin in infancy: "We never get a chance to find out whether we have any that are innate or not." *Mark Twain and Huck Finn* (Berkeley, Univ. of Calif. Press, 1960), p. viii, p. 138.

16. *A Connecticut Yankee in King Arthur's Court*, begun on the heels of *Huckleberry Finn*, in 1886, was Twain's next published book (December, 1889).

17. James Cox, in *Mark Twain: The Fate of Humor* (Princeton, Princeton Univ. Press, 1960), sees the ending specifically as an act of revenge on the audience. Moreover, Huck has never been anyone but a figure who sought escape from all moral commitments – good as well as bad. In my thinking, this is to read the book backwards, a dangerous practice. Perhaps this was what Twain's despair finally brought him to, but for the first two-thirds of this book, the alternative personal relationship with Jim, how-

ever fragile, does generate another form of consciousness in Huck. Without his consequent inner conflict the story would have little dramatic force. For Cox's definition of Huck to prevail, the entire Huck–Jim relationship has to be discounted. And Cox, as well as later critics who follow this line of argument, does reduce the relationship to that of a simple flight.

18. DeVoto, *Mark Twain's America*, p. 40.
19. *A World Elsewhere*, p. 182. See also Tony Tanner, "The Literary Children of James and Clemens," *Nineteenth Century Fiction*, XVI (Dec., 1961), pp. 205–18. "Huck's loneliness is the measure of the extent of his involvement" in society. "Huck is searching for something society doesn't have to offer, and the enforced alternatives are capitulation or escape" (p. 212).
20. *A World Elsewhere*, p. 198.
21. Michael J. Hoffman, "Huck's Ironic Circle," *Georgia Review* 23, p. 316.
22. It has been pointed out that the Phelps farm reflects a cherished childhood memory of the farm of Mark Twain's uncle, John Quarles; cf. H. Smith, Intro., *Huckleberry Finn*, p. xi.
23. DeVoto, in *Mark Twain's America*, points out that up to the 1840s "American lawlessness towered everywhere on the border" of the river, p. 17. But it seems clear that like the issue of slavery, these perversions of justice are intended to point up attitudes of mind and forms of behavior that are endemic to American society at large.
24. *Strains of Discord*, p. 51.
25. T. S. Eliot, introduction to *Adventures of Huckleberry Finn* (New York, Chanticleer Press, 1950).
26. *Mr. Clemens and Mark Twain*, p. 307.
27. For a view which emphasizes only the kinship between the two books, see Nicolaus Mills, "Social and Moral Vision in *Great Expectations* and *Huckleberry Finn*," *Journal of American Studies*, IV (July, 1970), pp. 61–72.
28. *Great Expectations*, first pub. 1860–61; Angus Calder, ed. (New York, Penguin Books, 1965), p. 360. Hereafter, all page references will be included in text.
29. See note 15.
30. Wilson, "Dickens: The Two Scrooges" (1939); rpt. in *The Wound and The Bow* (Cambridge, MA, Riverside Press, 1941), pp. 56, 57.
31. Hardy, "Dickens: The Later Novels," *Writers and Their Work*, ed. Geoffrey Bullough (London, Longmans, Green and Co., 1968), p. 30.
32. See Wilson, above. He credits T. A. Jackson's early Marxist analysis of Dickens with this insight. See also *Writers and Their Work*, p. 11.
33. See DeVoto, "The Symbols of Despair," in *Mark Twain at Work*;

and H. N. Smith, *Mark Twain, The Development of a Writer* (Cambridge, MA, Belknap Press, 1962).

CHAPTER IV

Strether Unbound: The Selective Vision of Henry James's Ambassador

1. See *The Notebooks of Henry James*, ed. F. O. Matthiessen and Kenneth B. Murdock (Chicago, Univ. of Chicago Press, 1981) for recurring concern with the tragedy of the unlived life, e.g., pp. 184, 187; and for a précis of the Sturgis incident, which provided the kernel of this story, pp. 225, 226. Saul Rosenzweig, "The Ghost of Henry James," *Partisan Review* (Fall, 1944), pp. 436–53, discusses the power of this theme in James's own psychology.

2. *The Ambassadors*, ed. S. P. Rosenbaum, Norton Critical Edition (New York, W. W. Norton & Co., 1964), p. 341. All subsequent references will be to this edition, and page numbers will be included in parentheses within the text.

3. Preface to *The Ambassadors*, rpt. in *The Art of the Novel*, ed. R. P. Blackmur (New York, Scribners, 1962), p. 324.

4. *Ibid.*

5. Cf. respectively, Marianna Torgovnick, *Closure in the Novel*, p. 138; Quentin Anderson, *The American Henry James* (New Brunswick, Rutgers Univ. Press, 1957), p. 222; Robert Garis, "The Two Lambert Strethers," *Modern Fiction Studies* 7 (Winter, 1961–62), pp. 305–16; Frederick Crews, *The Tragedy of Manners: Moral Drama in the Later Novels of Henry James* (1957, rpt. Archon Books, 1971), p. 33; Oscar Cargill, "*The Ambassadors*: A New View," *PMLA* 75 (1960), pp. 439–52.

6. Cf. Torgovnick, *Closure*: "In their final conversation, Strether sees most clearly, anticipates meanings, and verbally leads the way" (p. 138).

7. Whicher, p. 41.

8. Emerson, "Self-Reliance," Whicher, p. 160. "The populace think that your rejection of popular standard is a rejection of all standard and 'mere antinomianism' . . . But the law of consciousness abides." For Emerson, "consciousness" is direct awareness of a higher truth, eternal law.

9. Coleridge's famous distinction between imagination and fancy may be useful to consider here. In *Biographia Literaria*, Chapter III, he says, imagination is the power that "dissolves, diffuses, dissipates, in order to recreate . . ."; while Fancy depends upon "fixities and definites." "The Fancy is indeed no other than a mode of memory emancipated from the order of time and space."

1817; rpt. in David Perkins, ed. *English Romantic Writers* (New York, Harcourt, Brace, World, Inc., 1967), p. 452. Thus conceived, Strether is a man of Fancy, his hoard of impressions ultimately a substitute for his lack of imaginative power.

10. The phrase is used by Frank Kermode in *The Sense of an Ending*, p. 29.
11. James, quoted in Tony Tanner, *The Reign of Wonder* (Cambridge Univ. Press, 1965), p. 266.
12. *The Notebooks of Henry James*, p. 226.
13. Victor Turner, *The Forest of Symbols* (Ithaca, Cornell Univ. Press, 1967), p. 45. Turner's description of liminality as a *'rite de passage'* has interesting parallels to Strether's state, as it does to that of each of the protagonists discussed here.
14. Walter Pater, *The Renaissance* (New York, The Modern Library, no. pub. date, dedication date, 1873), xxv.
15. David Bromwich, "The Genealogy of Disinterestedness," *Raritan* (Spring, 1982), pp. 62–92, distinguishes between Arnold's version of this phrase and Pater's. For Arnold, to see "the object in itself" was to claim a genuine objectivity and impartiality for the viewer. What the viewer saw everyone could see. Pater responded by stressing the earlier Romantic acceptance of "realities" rather than a "reality." But while he acknowledged the solipsism inherent in the viewer's individual response, he feared it as "a shattering truth of spirit" (p. 87). He was caught, says Bromwich, in the trap of defining his own impressions by a realistic standard, as if there were a certitude beyond ourselves. (Strether's, and James's, need to provide himself with a moral as well as an aesthetic certitude might be seen as one strategy for evading this trap.)
16. Pater, xxvi.
17. Sallie Sears, *The Negative Imagination: Form and Perspective in the Novels of Henry James* (Ithaca, Cornell Univ. Press, 1968), p. ix. Says Sears, Europe and America represent two violently antithetical styles of life. At the end "each has operated on the other with something of the effect of a slow poison" (p. 111). Cf. Tony Tanner, "The Watcher from the Balcony: Henry James's *The Ambassadors,*' *Critical Quarterly*, 8 (Spring, 1966), pp. 35–52. Our last glimpse of Strether is "somehow out of life, but full of priceless vision" (p. 51); and Frederick Crews, *The Tragedy of Manners*: "Neither Woollett . . . nor Paris . . . can account for the sense of life that Strether has achieved through the expansion of his social and moral awareness" (p. 55).
18. Sears, *Negative Imagination*, p. ix.
19. Emery Elliott, *Revolutionary Writers: Literature and Authority in the New Republic* (New York, Oxford Univ. Press, 1982), p. 21. Elliott discusses the persistence and transformation of the

Calvinist millennial vision in the works of pre- and post-Revolutionary writers. And he also traces the line of a cultural tradition which extends from the eighteenth to the twentieth centuries.

20. Strether's willed naiveté is introduced as a feature of his character as early as his first London evening with Miss Gostrey. When he remarks that as compared with the vulgar business life of Woollett, the London theater is "divine," Miss Gostrey responds with surprise: "The dreadful . . . theatre? It's impossible, if you really want to know!" "Oh then . . . I *don't* really want to know!" he declares, p. 48.

21. Whicher, p. 149.

22. Frederick Crews, for instance, has found that the ending offers a vision of social inclusiveness and wholeness – a point of view that counsels a tolerance which borders on Christian love. *Tragedy of Manners*, p. 33.

23. *The Notebooks of Henry James*, p. 413.

24. Stephen Donadio, *Nietzsche, Henry James and the Artistic Will* (New York, Oxford Univ. Press, 1978), p. 82.

25. Strether's choice of images to define to himself the quality of his willed innocence suggests just how convoluted his defenses against reality actually are. For when has he ever so mocked and diminished both himself and Madame de Vionnet as in this self-castrating description? Turning the thought of this intimacy over in his mind, "he almost blushed, in the dark, for the way he had dressed the possibilities in vagueness, as a little girl might have dressed her doll" (p. 313).

26. Cf. Anderson, *The American Henry James*, p. 215: Strether never sees "the great simplicity that we are our own fate; that it is with ourselves we do battle."

27. Dorothea Krook, *The Ordeal of Consciousness in Henry James* (Cambridge, Cambridge Univ. Press, 1963), pp. 369, 333, argues that by the time that James wrote *The Ambassadors* he had overcome his own fear of the violence in sexual passion and recognized that passion is the source for all creative endeavor. "The Beast in the Jungle," which he was writing simultaneously with *The Ambassadors*, expresses the same recognition. James's work certainly reveals a preoccupation with this relation, but whether and how he dealt with it in his own life seems a separate and far more complex psychological issue than what Strether understands and does. That Strether may represent aspects of his creator (how could he not?), surely doesn't make them interchangeable figures.

28. See Tanner, note 17.

29. *The Notebooks of Henry James*, p. 227.

30. *The Notebooks*, p. 207.

31. *Art of the Novel*, p. 203.
32. *Puritan Origins*, p. 175.
33. See, for example, Lawrence Holland, *The Expense of Vision* (Princeton, Princeton Univ. Press, 1964): "Strether's folly" enacts the affair of art, the affair of memory and imagination . . . the exploitive sacrifice on which the novel is founded." His renunciation "is a substitute for the payment that might be made in the life of the emotions . . ." (p. 281). R. P. Blackmur, "The Loose and Baggy Monsters of Henry James,' in *Studies in Henry James*, ed. Veronica Makowsky (New York, New Directions, 1983); but also intro. to *The Golden Bowl* (New York, Dell, 1963), p. viii.
34. *Revolutionary Writers*, p. 8.
35. *Ibid.*, p. 95.
36. *Ibid.*, p. 8.
37. Cf. Newton Arvin's impassioned response to this moral crippling in *Hawthorne*, quoted in Matthiessen, *The American Renaissance* (New York, Oxford Univ. Press, 1941), p. 343: "What have been our grand national types of personality? The explorer . . . the Protestant sectarian . . . the freebooter and the smuggler . . . the pioneer . . . the philosophic anarchist in his hut in the woods . . . the economic individualist and the captain of industry: the go-getter, the tax-dodger, the bootlegger. The best and the worst of humanity . . . united after all in their common distrust of centrality . . . their domination by spiritual pride. United . . . finally in paying the penalty for disunion – in becoming partial and lopsided personalities, men and women of one dimension, august or vulgar cranks."
38. F. R. Leavis, *The Great Tradition* (1948; rpt. New York, N.Y. Univ. Press, 1963), pp. 163, 161.
39. For a view that concentrates on James's criticism of Strether, see Anderson, *The American Henry James*.
40. *The Renaissance*, p. 196.

CHAPTER V
Closing the Circle: *The Great Gatsby*

1. "Self-Reliance," *Selections from Ralph Waldo Emerson*, ed. Stephen Whicher, p. 166.
2. See Quentin Anderson, *The Imperial Self*, p. 33, for a clarifying discussion of the early Emerson to whom I refer.
3. Whicher, p. 157.
4. *Ibid.*, p. 101.
5. From "History," cited in Robert D. Richardson, Jr., "Emerson on History," *Harvard English Studies*, ed. Joel Porte (Cambridge, MA, Harvard Univ. Press, 1982), p. 59.
6. Whicher, p. 135.

7. *Ibid.*, p. 501. Richardson emphasizes that Emerson's view of history is based on his principle of the "essential identity of human nature in all ages and places"; that Emerson was very well read in the historical writing and scholarship of his own day; and that he sought for "a theory of history compatible with democracy" (pp. 53, 55, 60). See the full essay for an analysis that reaches some very different conclusions about Emerson than those suggested in my discussion.

8. Whicher, p. 56.

9. *Ibid.*, p. 55.

10. Brian M. Barbour, "*The Great Gatsby* and The American Past" *The Southern Review* (Spring, 1973), pp. 288–99, notes that Emerson's "whole career was a quarrel with the Franklinian spirit and the Franklinian dream" (p. 293). See also Quentin Anderson's discussion of "visionary capitalism" in "Property and Vision in Nineteenth-Century America," *The Virginia Quarterly Review*, 54 (Summer, 1978), pp. 385–410. Anderson believes this phenomenon to be provoked by the "psychically invasive character of a society in which self-definition had come close to being reduced to the quest for property," leading to the claim of "a more inclusive kind of property in vision itself."

11. Whicher, p. 23.

12. For a valuable discussion of the significance of market metaphors in Emerson's work see Michael T. Gilmore, "Emerson and the Persistence of Commodity," *Harvard English Studies*, #10, ed. Joel Porte (Cambridge, MA, Harvard Univ. Press, 1982), pp. 65–84.

13. Whicher, p. 22.

14. *The Great Gatsby* (1925; rpt. New York, Charles Scribner & Sons, 1953), p. 182. All subsequent references will be to this edition, and page numbers will be included in parentheses within the text.

15. Henry Dan Piper, *F. Scott Fitzgerald: A Critical Portrait* (New York, Holt, Rinehart & Winston, 1965). In the book's first draft the lament for the continent's innocence was originally to have concluded Chapter I, directly following the revelation of Daisy's "contamination" in tolerating Tom's infidelities. Later it was moved to Chapter IX, p. 108. Piper's information suggests that in its original design the identification of Daisy with the continent was virtually allegorical.

16. Robert Emmet Long, *The Achieving of the Great Gatsby: F. Scott Fitzgerald 1920–25* (Lewisburg, Bucknell Univ. Press, 1979), p. 140. "Fitzgerald uses time to dramatize and complement his theme, by having the novel proceed forward by simultaneously moving further and further back into the past, to the ultimate sources of illusion."

17. Alan Trachtenberg, "The Journey Back: Myth and History in *Tender is the Night*" in *Experience in the Novel*, ed. Roy Harvey Pearce (New York, Columbia Univ. Press, 1968), pp. 134–5.
18. R. W. Stallman, "Gatsby and The Hole in Time," *The Houses that James Built and Other Literary Studies* (East Lansing, Mich. State Univ. Press, 1964), p. 132.
19. For two views, among many, of Gatsby mythography see Bruce Michelson, "The Myth of Gatsby," *Modern Fiction Studies*, 26 (Winter, 1980–81), pp. 563–78; and Peter L. Hays, "Gatsby, Myth, Fairy Tale and Legend," *Southern Folklore Quarterly*, #40 (1977), pp. 213–33.
20. Richard Hofstadter, *The American Political Tradition* (New York, Vintage, 1974), p. xxxv. "But beginning with the time of Bryan, the dominant American ideal has been steadily fixed on bygone institutions and conditions. In early twentieth-century progressivism this backward-looking vision reached the dimensions of a major paradox. Such heroes of the progressive revival as Bryan, La Follette, and Wilson proclaimed that they were trying to undo the mischief of the past forty years and re-create the old nation of limited and decentralized power, genuine competition, democratic opportunity and enterprise." It is noteworthy that this backward-looking vision which Hofstadter found in political rhetoric appeared in our literature at least as early as Cooper's Leatherstocking Tales. There is work to be done as well in enlarging our understanding of the historical grounds that conditioned Emerson's own vision.
21. Alan Trachtenberg, *The Incorporation of America* (New York, Hill & Wang, 1982), p. 82. Even as English social philosopher Herbert Spencer's Social Darwinism was being used to justify business success as a law of nature, new forms of monopoly capitalism that depended upon doing away with competition were taking shape. "Increasingly, the instrument of success proved to be more effective organization, the restructuring of enterprises into corporations in which financing and sales along with production fell under control of a single entity." Though proclaimed as an age of individualism, actually there was a "decisive decline of proprietors, family businesses, simple partnerships: the familiar forms of capital."
22. Cf. Emerson's "History": We honor the rich "because they have externally the freedom, power and grace which we feel to be proper to man, proper to us." Quoted in Robinson, p. 58. John Peale Bishop, "The Missing All," *Virginia Quarterly Review*, #13 (1937), pp. 106–22, seems to have been among the first to note the affinity with Emerson. He remarks that Gatsby is "the Emersonian Man brought to completion and eventually to failure ..." (p. 115).

23. Piper, *A Critical Portrait*, notes that in the earliest draft of *The Great Gatsby* "Nick and Gatsby are so alike in temperament that it was only after extensive revision that Fitzgerald succeeded in endowing them with separate personalities" (p. 107).

24. A. B. Paulson, "*The Great Gatsby*: Oral Aggression and Splitting." *American Imago*, #35 (1978), p. 311–30. In this psychoanalytic interpretation, Nick's self-division is defined as a regressive, pre-Oedipal solution to ambiguity, characterized by a rigid morality of good or bad, clean or dirty; not an acceptance of real complexity but an affirmation of opposites, p. 330.

25. Cf. Nick's description of Wilson's garage when Tom first takes him there to meet his girl. "It had occurred to me that this shadow of a garage must be a blind, and that sumptuous and romantic apartments were concealed overhead, when the proprietor himself appeared in the door of an office, wiping his hands on a piece of waste" (p. 25).

26. Piper, *Portrait*, quotes a letter to Ludlow Fowler written while Fitzgerald was finishing the first draft of the book. "That's the burden of this novel, the loss of those illusions that give such color to the world that you don't care whether things are true or false so long as they partake of the magical glory" (p. 106).

27. Henry Dan Piper sees Nick's traditional, inherited values as saving him from "Gatsby's terrible mistake"; sending him back home to take up "his responsibilities as a member of the Carraway clan" and grow up (p. 111). Arthur Mizener, in "The Poet of Borrowed Time," *F. Scott Fitzgerald: The Man and His Work*, ed. Alfred Kazin (New York, Collier Books, 1967), pp. 23–45, sees the East as representing corruption and sophistication and culture; the West as representing the simple moral virtue of Nick and Gatsby. James Tuttleton, in *The Novel of Manners in America* (Chapel Hill, Univ. of North Carolina Press, 1972), p. 179, says: "Nick's return to the Midwest is a return to the origins of his existence, to the wisdom of his father, to the middle-class 'fundamental decencies' marked by the inner check, by the family noted through generations in the same place, by social stability." These critics apparently read the prologue without noticing the ironies and contradictions in Nick's portrait of himself. Nor do they consider it in relation to Nick's subsequent remarks about the Midwest and his assertion to Gatsby that you can't repeat the past, can't go home again.

28. Malcolm Cowley, "F. Scott Fitzgerald: The Romance of Money," *The Western Review* (Summer, 1953), p. 245. Cowley notes the relation between money and vitality or potency.

29. Bercovitch, *Puritan Origins*, pp. 145–6, emphasizes the distinction between the classical theory of *translatio studii* – civilization moving in a "westward course" – based on a cyclical view of

history, and the American transmutation of it. Here, the rise and fall of empire is recast as redemptive history, with America as mankind's "last act in the drama of salvation." Though this initially was the work of Puritan theorists, Bercovitch finds its effect consistent throughout nineteenth-century American thought. Fitzgerald, who was well-read in American history, would seem to have intuited the same attitude toward his country's moral promise and moral failure as he found in those works whose conventions form the body of his own consciously allusive text.

30. Lionel Trilling, commenting on *The Professor's House* by Willa Cather, inadvertently provides an apt summary of Nick's condition. (Cather is an author Fitzgerald is known to have admired.) He says that, whatever its failings, the book "epitomizes ... the disgust with life which so many sensitive Americans feel, which makes them dream of their preadolescent integration and innocent community with nature, speculate on the 'release from effort' and the 'eternal solitude' of death; and eventually reconcile themselves to a life 'without delight.' " "Willa Cather," rpt. in *After the Genteel Tradition*, 1910–1930, ed. Malcolm Cowley (Carbondale, Southern Illinois Press, 1936), p. 52.

31. Arthur Mizener, *The Far Side of Paradise* (Boston, Houghton Mifflin, 1951), p. 177, while praising the book's skill and power notes that it "never suggests a point of view which might bring seriously into question the adequacy to experience" of its depiction of Gatsby's glamour, his "heightened sensitivity to the promises of life." I am glad to find this subject broached in what was the earliest, and still seems the best, critical biography we have of Fitzgerald.

32. John W. Aldridge, "The Life of Gatsby" in *Twelve Original Essays on Great American Novels*, ed. Charles Shapiro (Detroit, Wayne State Press, 1958), p. 228. This essay expresses a standard view which endorses Gatsby's antinomian qualities. Comparing his immorality to that of the Buchanans, Aldridge says, "Theirs is a fundamental lawlessness of the heart ... His is the lawlessness of the merely illegal and is excusable on the ground of the service it renders in enforcing the highest laws of the heart." One wonders if Aldridge intended these "highest laws" to include the putative murder as well as Gatsby's complicity in manslaughter.

33. See Alan Heimert and Perry Miller, *The Great Awakening* (New York, Bobbs-Merrill Co., 1967), p. ii, note 15.

34. Long, *The Achieving of Gatsby*, pp. 158–9. "Like certain Greek pastorals, it has the nature of a lament or elegy for a dead friend ... at the end [Gatsby] has been evoked as a slain god, a youthful deity of spring, or a morning light, sacrificed to the

progression of time. His death suggests a ritualistic sacrifice."
Thus we can see more clearly here than anywhere else in the
novel, Nick's role as the creator (not merely the observer) of
Gatsby's mythic status.

35. One example of the critical bind to which the dismissal of Nick
can lead is Richard Forster's "The Way to Read *Gatsby*," in *Sense
and Sensibility in Twentieth-Century Writing*, ed. Brom Weber
(Carbondale, Southern Illinois Univ. Press, 1970), pp. 94–108.
Forster distrusts Nick, yet wants to keep the affirmation he gives
us in the ending. He likens Nick to Dowell, the neurotic narrator
of Ford's *The Good Soldier*, saying that Nick masks neurotic
curiosity in tenderness of feeling. Chronically fearful, he is, like
Dowell, the modern impotent man. Yet "even Nick's own wishful version of beautiful futility recognizes the continual
phoenix-rebirth of dream and aspiration as the fountainhead
of human history" (p. 108). The "even" is surprising. How, in
this portrait, do we know that Nick's recognition of the
"fountainhead" isn't meant ironically, that the "phoenix-
rebirth" is not neurotic compensation for his personal
impotence? Forster needs some touchstone of integrity for
Nick, if he is to salvage any meaning from the book, but he never
clarifies the boundary between Nick's supposed falsity and the
authenticity of his commitment to Gatsby's vision.

36. The majority of critics take this view of Nick's role, placing it in
the tradition of the European initiation story and so reading the
ending as a hard-won acceptance of the lessons of experience –
precisely that accommodation to "reality" which I believe Fitzgerald's ending resists. William Troy's comment, in "Scott
Fitzgerald – The Authority of Failure," Kazin, ed. *The Man and
His Work*, is representative. He sees Nick's experience as a
record of "the strenuous passage from deluded youth to
maturity" (p. 191).

37. Wayne Booth, *The Rhetoric of Fiction* (Chicago, Univ. of
Chicago Press, 1961, 1983), p. 346.

38. See James E. Miller, Jr., *F. Scott Fitzgerald: His Art and Tech-
nique* (New York, N.Y. Univ. Press, 1964), p. 92; Robert
Emmet Long, "*The Great Gatsby* and the Tradition of Joseph
Conrad," *Texas Studies in Language and Literature*, VIII
(Summer, 1966), pp. 257–76; (Fall, 1966), pp. 407–22.

39. Joseph Conrad, *Selected Stories* (New York, Doubleday Doran
& Co., 1930), p. 85. All subsequent references will be to this
edition and page numbers will be included in parentheses
within the text.

40. The passage reads: "But Marlow was not typical . . . and to him
the meaning of an episode was not inside like a kernel but outside, enveloping the tale which brought it out only as a glow

brings out a haze, in the likeness of one of these misty halos that sometimes are made visible by the spectral illumination of moonshine" (p. 48).

41. Trachtenberg, *Incorporation*, p. 180.

42. Milton Stern, *The Golden Moment* (Urbana, Univ. of Illinois Press, 1970), p. 238. "On every social level in the novel, the overwhelming and constant lesson of America is that without wealth one is in the precariousness and peril of constantly being 'Mr. Nobody from Nowhere' . . . And the parallels between all levels are constantly made visible."

43. Malcolm Cowley, "The Scott Fitzgerald Story," *New Republic* (Feb. 12, 1951), pp. 17–20, relates the social changes in the twenties to the shift from production to consumption ethic. The older emphasis on saving and self-denial, in order to accumulate capital for new enterprise, gives way to the encouragement to buy and enjoy, "in order to provide markets for new products endlessly streaming from the production lines."

44. Whicher, p. 61.

45. Cf. Emerson, 'Nature': "We are taught by great actions that the universe is the property of every individual in it. Every rational creature has all nature for his dowry and estate. . . . In proportion to the energy of his thought and will, he takes up the world into himself." Whicher, p. 29.

46. Trachtenberg, *Incorporation*, pp. 145–6. The healing properties of high culture were associated with women and their role as anodyne for masculine aggression; women were seen to represent non-material values, non-aggressive, non-exploitative. Horace Bushnell's 1869 tract against women's rights, *Women's Suffrage: The Reform Against Nature*, called women "the beauty principle" as opposed to "the force principle" of men. He argued that participation in the civil realm would corrupt feminine character.

47. Emerson, "Wealth," quoted in Gilmore, p. 81. Gilmore notes that by the time of the Civil War Emerson was increasingly unable to distinguish between "natural law and the market regime"; that *laissez-faire* takes on spiritual connotations, until in "Wealth" he repudiates his early radical thought and "glorifies worldly success as a sign of spiritual election."

48. In May, 1925, one month after the book's publication, Fitzgerald wrote to Mencken acknowledging the "tremendous fault in . . . the lack of an emotional presentment of Daisy's attitude toward Gatsby after their reunion . . . no one has spotted it because it's concealed beneath elaborate and overlapping blankets of prose." Stern, p. 182.

CONCLUSION

1. Michael Paul Rogin, *Subversive Genealogy: The Politics and Art of Herman Melville* (Berkeley, Univ. of Calif. Press, 1979).
2. Herman Melville, *Moby-Dick*, eds. Harrison Hayford and Hershel Parker, Norton Critical Edition (New York, W. W. Norton & Co., 1967), p. 59. All references will be from this edition and page numbers hereafter included in parentheses within the text.
3. Paul Brodtkorb, Jr., *Ishmael's White World* (New Haven and London, Yale Univ. Press, 1965), p. 52.
4. Charles Feidelson, Jr., *Symbolism and American Literature* (Chicago, Univ. of Chicago Press, 1953), p. 31.
5. Hans Myerhoff, *Time in Literature* (Berkeley, Univ. of Calif. Press, 1955), p. 48.
6. Ursula Brumm, "Non-Conformity and Wilderness in Cotton Mather, *Prospects: Annual of American Culture Studies*, ed. Jack Salzman, Vol. 6 (1981), pp. 1–15.

Index

Index

Index

Tocqueville, Alexis de 25, 39
Trachtenberg, Alan 104, 106, 121
  Incorporation of America 106
Trilling, Lionel 8, 31, 145 n. 10, 155 n. 30
Trollope, Anthony 8
Turner, Victor 149 n. 13
Twain, Mark 13, 46–74 *passim*, 125, 127, 137
  Connecticut Yankee 56
  Huckleberry Finn 9, 12, 46–74

Uncle Tom's Cabin 54
Updike, John 128

Warren, Robert Penn 49
"Wealth" 157 n. 47
Whitman, Walt 4, 57
Whittier, John Greenleaf 51
Wilson, Edmund 71
Winthrop, John 32
Wuthering Heights 41

"Young Goodman Brown" 7, 24